古 文 今 译 与 英 译

Classical Chinese — Present-Day Chinese and English Renditionss

编译　冯树鉴

华 语 教 学 出 版 社
北 京

SINOLINGUA　BEIJING

First Edition 1990

Second Printing 2000

ISBN 7-80052-149-4

Copyright 2000 by Sinolingua

Published by Sinolingua

24 Baiwanzhuang Road, Beijing 100037, China

Tel: (86) 10-68994599 / 68326333

Fax: (86) 10-68326642

E-mail: sinolingua@ihw.com.cn

Printed by Beijing Foreign Languages Printing House

Distributed by China International

Book Trading Corporation

35 Chegongzhuang Xilu, P.O. Box 399

Beijing 100044, China

Printed in the People's Republic of China

序 言

冯树鉴先生长期从事外语教学和中外语言的修辞研究，在古汉语、现代汉语和外语三方面都有较高的造诣。此次，编写《古文今译与英译》一书，所选文言文，都是文字简短、含意隽永的精品；译写的现代文，忠于原意，通俗流畅；英语译文浅显传神，读起来朗朗上口，富有节奏感和音韵美。对一些词语还加了准确简明的注释。这本读物既适合于国内大、中学生欣赏古文、阅读英文，又能够满足国内外研习汉语者学习汉语文言文的需要。总之，这本读物犹如一座桥梁，不仅在时间上沟通古今，还从空间上沟通中外，是外语教学中的一种有益的尝试，很值得一读。

潘庆云　1989 年于上海

自　序

目前世界上有十亿多人用英语，也有十亿多人用汉语。因此，英汉互译是全世界最重要的翻译之一。翻译是艺术(art)、技巧(craft)和科学(science)三者的综合。此外还涉及到风格(style)问题。古文有古文的风格，如常有重复(repetition)。在古文英译中，"repetition"不显累赘时，不妨重复，以求"信"于古文风格。例如《三戒》一文中，"戒之在色"，"戒之在斗"，"戒之在得"，译成"avoid lust"，"avoid bandying"，"avoid greed"。不如此，就很难再现古文中的"repetition"。总的说来，古文用词精练，因此，英译文也须"精练"一些，以求"达"和"雅"于古文风格。

汉语讲究"排比"或"对仗"，因此，古文英译要注意到词语搭配的平衡问题。例如《三友》，《三乐》，《三戒》中，古文词语整齐匀称，抑扬顿挫，十分和谐，富韵律感。有位西洋人把"乐骄乐，乐佚游，乐宴乐"译成"To enjoy oneself in false pride, in sauntering and in feasting"，就失去排比、对仗的节奏感了。

另外，古文英译中句法问题也很重要。《三友》，《三乐》，《三戒》这三段古文，包括七个复句，其中三十个分句，分句与分句之间的连接，无一个连词，这是古汉语的特点之一。但英语则相反，多用连词或关联词。如《三友》英译文中，共有六个关联词 who 来承上启下；又如《三戒》英译文中，共用三个连词 when 来衔接上下文，这是符合英语句法特点的。

再有，古文今译，不但要熟悉文言修辞，注意题旨和语境，而且还要仔细琢磨并辨清楚含蓄深蕴的词义。例如"乐骄乐"，这里的"骄"，上述那个西洋人误解为"骄傲"（译成 false pride）；但实际上指的是"放纵"之意。

本书分为"立志篇"、"求知篇"、"人才篇"、"德性篇"、"教化篇"、"哲理篇"、"智愚篇"、"悔改篇"、"讽喻篇"等。这只是大略分类，为了各有所属，便于读者阅读，并无一定道理，也不一定恰当。书中中、英文都做有简单注释，供读者参考。《古文今译与英译》力求在古今中外的文化窗口方面能起铺路搭桥、沟通交流的作用，并在接受、继承和对外传播祖国文化遗产以及对外汉语教学方面有所裨益。按照这样的要求，本书只是起了一个头，作了一次抛砖引玉的粗浅的尝试，犹如浩瀚的译海中溅射出的几朵浪花而已。

在编译过程中，同济大学美国专家 Lucinda Lawrence 等对我热诚指教，谨在此致以衷心的感谢。笔者学识浅薄，经验短缺，书中难免有不妥和错误，诚恳地希望读者给予指正。

冯树鉴　　1989 年于上海

目 录
Contents

立 志 篇

The Chapter of Ambition

大鹏之志

蜩①与学鸠②笑之曰:"我决起而飞,枪③榆枋而止;时则不正,而控④于地已矣。奚以⑤九万里而南为?"……之二虫又何知!

——《庄子》

[今译]

(大海那边有一只叫鹏的大鸟,一飞就是九万里……。海滩上)有只小蝉和一只叫斑鸠的小鸟,看着鹏的那股劲头,讥笑说:"我们什么时候愿意飞,就一下子飞起来;碰到榆树、枋树,就停落在上面;有时力气不够,飞不动,就落下地来算了。嘻,鹏啊!哪里用得着飞到九万里高再向南飞(那么

---

① 蜩 tiáo:蝉
② 学鸠:一种小鸟
③ 枪:触,碰上
④ 控:投,落下
⑤ 奚以……为:哪里用得着……呢?古汉语中表示反问的一种习惯用法。

远）呢？……小蝉和小斑鸠,怎么能理解大鹏的志向呵!

[英译]

The Ambition① of a Roc②

Across the ocean there was a bird of great size called a roc, who upon taking flight, flew over ninety thousand miles at a stretch. On the beach there was a cicada③and a turtle—dove④, who looked at the vigour⑤of the roc and said in a sarcastic⑥voice:

"If we want to take flight, we simply fly up into the air. When we come across⑦an elm⑧or a sandal⑨, we stop there for a rest. At times we

---

①ambition　n. 志向,抱负

②roc　n. 大鹏

③cicada　n. 蝉

④turtle—dove　n. 斑鸠

⑤vigour　n. 活力,精力

⑥sarcastic　adj. 讽刺的,挖苦的,嘲笑的

⑦come　across (越过…而)来到;(偶然)遇见

⑧elm　n. 榆木

⑨sandal　n. 檀木

run out of strength, and we come down to the earth. Oh! My dear roc, what need is there to fly as high as ninety thousand miles up before flying toward the South?"

How could they know the ambition of the roc?

蜀鄙之僧

[古文]

　　蜀之鄙① 有二僧:其一贫,其一富。贫者语于富者曰:"吾欲之南海,何如?"富者曰:"子何恃② 而往?"曰:"吾一瓶一钵③ 足矣。"富者曰:"吾数年来欲买舟而下,犹未能也;子何恃而往?"越明年④,贫者自南海还,以告富者,富者有惭色。西蜀之去南海,不知几千里也。 僧之富者不能至,而贫者至焉。 人之立志,顾不如蜀鄙之僧哉!

——彭端淑 《白鹤堂集》

[今译]

　　四川郊野有两个僧人:一个穷,一个富。穷僧对富僧说:"我想去南海,怎么样?"富僧说:"您靠什么前去?"穷僧说:"我带一个水瓶,一个饭钵就够

――――――――

①鄙:边远的地方
②恃:依靠
③钵:佛教徒盛饭的用具。
④越明年:越:到。明年:第二年。

了。"富僧说："我几年来想雇船向下游走,尚且不能实现;您靠什么去呢?"到了第二年,穷僧从南海回来,告诉富僧,富僧感到羞愧。四川距离南海,不知有几千里远,富僧不能到达,而穷僧却到达了。人们的立志,反而不如四川郊野的僧人啊!

[英译]

Two Monks① in the Frontier

of Sichuan

There lived two monks in the frontier② of Sichuan: one poor and the other rich. One day the poor monk said to the rich one:

"I'm thinking of going to Nanhai. What do you think of it?"

"On what do you depend for going there?" asked the rich monk. "A bottle and a basin③ will

---

①monk   n. 和尚,僧侣
②frontier   n. 边远地区
③basin   n. 钵,盆

suffice①me," answered the other.

"Well, I have been entertaining②the idea of taking a boat and setting off for there for many years, but have failed thus far. How can you go without any support?"

One year later the poor monk returned from Nanhai and told his travels to the rich one, who was put to shame③to hear it.

It is so many thousand miles from the frontier of Sichuan to Nanhai. The rich monk failed to go, but the poor one went. Couldn't we make up our minds④to do something as the poor monk of the frontier of Sichuan did?

---

①suffice   v.t. 满足…的需要
②entertain   v.t. 准备考虑,心中存有
③shame   n. 羞愧,羞耻
④make up one's mind 下决心

岳飞分赐沉香

[古文]

王一日，以沉香① 分属官，各得一块，而黄机密② 所得最小；以为不均，复以一裹分之，而机密所得复小，王怃然③。机密曰："某以一身从军，虽得香，无所用之。"王乃曰："某旧日亦爱烧香，瓦炉中烧柏香耳，后来亦屏④ 之。大丈夫欲立功业，岂可有所好耶！"众有愧色。

——黄元振 《百氏昭忠录》

[今译]

有一天，岳飞把沉香分赐给属下的官员，每人都获得了一块。而主管档案的黄纵所得到的最小。岳飞觉得分得不太均匀，又将一包裹的沉香分给大家，可是黄纵得到的仍旧是最小的。 岳飞

---

①沉香：一种植物，学名"伽南香"，是一种名贵香料。
②机密：主管机密事务的官名。此指保管档案的官。
③怃然：怅然失意的样子。
④屏：退避，放弃。

总觉得未合自己的心意。黄纵说:"我只身投军,即使分到沉香,也没有什么用处。"岳飞就说:"我过去也喜欢烧香,只是在瓦炉中烧一些普通的柏香,后来就不烧了。男子汉要为国家建立功勋,怎么能老是想着个人的爱好呢!"大家都露出惭愧的表情。

[英译]

Yue Fei Distributing[①]

Aloeswood Incense[②]

One day General Yue Fei distributed aloeswood incense to his officers, and each of them got a share[③]of it. Because the archivist[④]in charge of secret documents, Huang Zong, took the smallest part, Yue Fei thought it was an

---

①distribute v.t. 分发,分配: They distributed the newspapers to all the houses in the city. 他们把报纸送给市里所有的住户。

②aloeswood incense　n. 沉香

③share　n. 一份

④archivist　n. 管理档案的职员

unfair division①. He distributed another parcel② of aloeswood incense to everybody. Huang Zong still got the smallest one which Yue Fei considered far from satisfactory.

"I have devoted my life to the service of the military," said Huang Zong. "Though I have aloeswood incense, it is useless to me."

"I used to like burning joss—sticks③," said Yue Fei. "In fact, I used to burn the common cypress④kind in an earthenware⑤censer⑥, but I have since given it up. A person who is filled with ambition should always do service to his country first. How can he think about personal interests all the time?" At this everyone felt ashamed.

---

①division n. 分配,分派：(the) division of labour 分工
②parcel n. 包裹
③joss—stick n. 香
④cypress n. 柏属植物
⑤earthenware n. 陶器
⑥censer n. 香炉

张溥抄书

[古文]

溥幼嗜①学。所读书必手抄,抄已朗诵一过,即焚之,又抄,如是者六七始已。右手握管处,指掌成茧。冬日手皲,日沃②汤③数次,后名读书之斋曰"七录",以此也。……溥诗文敏捷。四方征索者,不起草,对客挥毫,俄顷④立就,以故名高一时。

——《明史·张溥传》

[今译]

张溥从小就酷爱学习。凡是所读的书一定要亲手抄写。抄后朗诵一遍,就把它烧掉,又重新抄写,像这样要六七次方才作罢。他右手握笔管的地方,手指和手掌都磨出了老茧。冬天手的皮肤

---

①嗜:喜欢,特殊的爱好。
②沃:灌溉,浇水。此指用水洗。
③汤:热水
④俄顷:不久,一会儿。

受冻皲裂，每天要在热水里洗好几次。后来他把读书的房间题名为"七录"，就是这个意思。……张溥写作思路敏捷。各个地方的人向他索取诗文，他从来不打草稿，当着来客的面，挥动毛笔，一会就写成，所以一时名声大噪。

[英译]

Zhang Pu Copying Books

Since childhood, Zhang Pu had been fond of learning. He always copied with his own hand every book he perused①, read it aloud once, and then burned the copy that he had made. What was more②, he didn't stop at making only one copy of a book but made six or seven copies. As a result, thick calluses ③appeared on his right hand from holding the writing brush④.

In winter his hands became chapped and

---

①peruse v.t. 阅读，细读
②what is more 而且，另外，更重要的是
③thick callus n. 老茧
④writing brush n. 毛笔

cracked①and he soaked②them in hot water several times every day. Then he named his study 'Seven Copies' meaning just that.

Zhang Pu had a very nimble③train of thought④when writing, and people came from near and far⑤asking for his poems and prose⑥. Without making a rough⑦sketch⑧ he moved his writing brush and finished his works in the visitors' presence⑨ in only a little while. Because of this he enjoyed tremendous popularity⑩ for a time.

---

①chapped and cracked 皲裂
②soak v.t. 浸泡
③nimble adj. 敏捷的，敏锐的
④train of thought 思路
⑤near and far 远近,到处
⑥prose n. 散文
⑦rough adj. 粗略的
⑧sketch n. 草图,略图
⑨in someone's presence = in the presence of someone 在…的
    面前
⑩enjoy tremendous popularity 享有崇高的声誉

赵广断指画观音

[古文]

赵广，合肥人，本李伯时家小史①。伯时作画，每使侍左右，久之遂善画，尤工作马，几能乱真。建炎中陷贼，贼闻其善画，使图②所掳妇人。广毅然辞以实不能画。胁以白刃，不从。逐断右手拇指遣去。而广平生实用左手。乱定，惟画观音大士③而已。又数年乃死。今士大夫所藏伯时观音，多广笔也。

——陆游《老学庵笔记》

[今译]

赵广，合肥人，原是北宋名画家李伯时家的书童。李伯时作画时，他常在旁边侍候，久而久之，他也善于作画了，尤其擅长画马，他画的马几乎可以同李伯时所画的真迹相混。宋高宗建炎年间，他

---

①小史：书童。
②图：画。
③大士：此指品质高尚的人。

不幸落入金兵之手。金兵听说他擅长作画,就叫他画被他们掳掠去的妇女。赵广毅然推辞,不肯作画。金兵用雪亮的刀子威胁他,他没有屈从。金兵就砍断他的右手拇指,打发他离开。然而,赵广平时作画实际上是左手。乱定之后,赵广就只画观音大士。又过了几年,他便去世了。现在士大夫所藏的伯时观音图,多数是赵广的手笔。

[英译]

Painting the Bodhisattva

Guanyin①with One

Thumb② Missing

Zhao Guang, a native of Hefei, had been a studio③—boy at the home of the famous painter Li Boshi during the Northern Song Dynasty. When Li Boshi was painting, the boy frequently

①the Bodhisattva Guanyin　观世音菩萨
②thumb　n. 拇指
③studio n. 画室,工作室

served at his side. Day after day he became better at painting as well, especially at painting horses, which were perfect enough to pass off as①Li Boshi's genuine②works.

During the reign③of the Emperor Song Gaozong (Jian'an), Zhao Kuo unfortunately fell into the hands of Jin soldiers. As they knew he was skillful at painting, they asked him to paint pictures of the women they had captured④. He declined⑤resolutely, refusing to paint for them. They then threatened⑥ him with gleaming⑦ knives, but he did not submit⑧, so they broke his right thumb off and ordered him to go away.

However, Zhao Guang was left-handed. After the disaster⑨, he painted only the

①pass off as, pass for 冒充为
②genuine adj. 真正的
③reign n. （君主的）统治时期
④capture v.t. 俘虏
⑤decline v.i. 辞谢
⑥threaten v.t. 恐吓,威胁
⑦gleam v.i. 闪光
⑧submit v.i. （使）屈服
⑨disaster n. 大灾难

Bodhisattva Guanyin. Some years later he passed away①.

Nowadays most of the pictures of the Bodhisattva Guanyin claimed② to be Boshi's maintained by bureaucratic scholars③ are actually Zhao Guang's paintings.

---

①pass away 去世
②claim　v.t.　声称,断言
③bureaucratic scholar　士大夫

小子安知壮士之志

[古文]

　　班超……为人有大志，不修细节。然内孝谨，居家常执勤苦，不耻劳辱。有口辩，而涉猎书传。

　　永平五年，兄固被召诣校书郎①，超与其母随至洛阳。

　　家贫，常为官佣书以供养。久劳苦，尝辍②业投笔叹曰："大丈夫无它志略，犹当效傅介子、张骞③立功异域，以取封侯，安能久事笔研间乎？"左右皆笑之，超曰："小子安知壮士志哉！"

　　　　——范晔　《后汉书·班超列传》

[今译]

　　班超……胸有大志，外表上不讲究小节，可是实际上孝顺谨慎。在家常常辛勤操作，从不厌恶体力劳动，能言善辩，并且读了不少古代书籍。

___

①校书郎：汉代的官名，主管书籍校勘。
②辍：停
③傅介子、张骞：汉代的官吏，曾出使西域。

汉永平五年,班超的哥哥班固被召赴校书郎任,班超与母亲跟随到了洛阳。家境贫困,班超就经常受官府雇佣抄书来供养母亲。长期辛勤劳作, 有一次停下工作把笔一扔,感叹说:"大丈夫没有别的志愿和谋划,还是当以傅介子、张骞为榜样在西域建立功勋,博取封侯,怎能长期生活在笔砚之间呢?"周围的人都笑话他,班超说:"你们这些人怎会理解壮士的雄心呢!"

[英译]

How Can You Possibly

Understand a Hero's Ambition?

Ban Chao who was filled with ambition was careless about his trifling①personal matters and appearance. In fact, he was filial②and circumspect③. He worked hard in the household, never

①trifling   adj. 不重要的,微不足道的
②filial   adj. 孝顺的,子女的
③circumspect   adj. 谨慎的,慎重的

finding physical labour repulsive①. He was skilled in both speech and argument②, for he read many ancient books.

In the 5th year of Yongping [62 A.D.],as his elder brother Ban Gu was appointed as a supreme official in charge of the state library, Ban Chao and his mother followed him and settled in the capital of Luo Yang too.

The want③of his family required that Ban Chao frequently copy books in the employment of local authorities to support himself and his mother. After labouring for quite a long time, he once stopped copying, and throwing his writing brush to the ground, sighed④out:

"If a real man has no other desire or plan, he had better follow Fu Jiezi and Zhang Qian's examples of establishing⑤ merit⑥ abroad and winning a high official post and favour upon re-

---

①repulsive　adj. 令人厌恶的
②argument　n.　辩论
③want　n. 贫困
④sigh　v.i. 叹气：sigh out 叹气地说
⑤establish　v.t.　建立
⑥merit　n. 功绩

turn. How can he misspend①his youth among writing brushes and inkstone year in and year out?" All his colleagues around laughed at him. Ban Chao said: "How can you possibly understand a hero's ambition!"

---

①misspend v.t. 虚度

求　知　篇

The Chapter of Learning

炳烛之光

[古文]

　　晋平公问于师旷曰："吾年七十，欲学恐已暮①矣。"师旷曰："何不炳烛乎？"平公曰："安有为人臣而戏其君乎？"师旷曰："盲臣安敢戏君乎？臣闻之：少而好学，如日出之阳；壮而好学，如日中之光；老而好学，如炳烛之明。孰与昧②行乎？"平公曰："善哉！"

——刘向　《说苑》

[今译]

　　有一次，晋平公对他的臣子师旷说："我年纪老了，都七十啦！很想学习，读些书，不过，又怕太晚了。"师旷说：" '太晚了'吗？为什么不点支蜡烛呢？"平公说："我跟你谈正经的，你倒同我开起玩笑来了。"师旷说："我这已瞎眼的臣子，怎敢跟大王开玩笑！我听说过：少年时期好学的人，他就象

---

①暮：此指晚。
②昧：暗

早晨的太阳,光芒四射;壮年时期好学的人,就象中午的太阳,灿烂辉煌。人到了老年,还能好学,就象点燃的一支蜡烛。虽然不怎么亮,但发出光来,总比黑暗一团要好多了吧!"

平公说:"你说得真好啊!"

[英译]

The Light of a Candle

One day Marquis①Ping of the State of Jin said to his minister Shikuang: "I'm seventy years old now. Though I desire②to read and learn more, I am afraid it may be too late. You see I'm in the evening of my life."

"In the evening? Then why don't you light a candle?"

"I have spoken to my minister in earnest and he in turn jests③with his lord ④."

---

①marquis　n. 侯爵
②desire　v.t.　想要,希望
③jest　v.i. 开玩笑
④lord　n. 君主

Shikuang said: "How dare I, a blind man? I have heard that a youth who is eager①in his studies has a bright future radiating light like the rising sun. A person of middle age, if he is keen②on his learning, just shines as the sun at high noon. A person of old age, if he is still given to③his study and reading, will give out light as much as a lighted candle does. In spite of its dim④light, it is far far better than pitch−dark⑤!"

"What you said is quite right," approved⑥ Marquis Ping admiringly.

---

①eager adj. 渴望,热衷于: eager for / after success 渴望成功; be very eager in one's studies 发愤求学
②keen adj. 渴望的,热心于: be keen about the trip 渴望能成行; be keen on going abroad 渴望出国
③be given to 使沉湎于…; 为…献身, 献出
④dim adj. 不亮的,朦胧的: eyes dim with tears 泪水模糊的眼睛
⑤pitch−dark adj. 漆黑
⑥approve v.i. (of) 批准,赞成

担薪诵书

[古文]

朱买臣……吴人也。家贫,好读书,不治产业,常艾① 薪樵,卖以给食。

担束薪,行且诵书。其妻亦负戴相随,数止买臣毋歌讴② 道中。买臣愈益疾歌。妻羞之,求去。

——《汉书·朱买臣传》

[今译]

朱买臣……吴县人。家里很穷,但他很喜欢读书,不懂理产谋生,常常去砍柴草,靠卖柴过活。

朱买臣挑着两捆柴,一边走,一边朗诵诗句。他的妻子也背着柴跟在后面,几次三番劝阻买臣不要在路上朗读,买臣却更加提高了嗓门。妻子觉得这是羞耻的事,便要求离婚。

---

①艾:通"刈"。割
②歌讴:歌唱;讴:歌曲。这里指用唱的形式诵诗。

Reading Aloud While Carrying Firewood

Zhu Maichen was a native① of the Wu County. He was very poor but fond of learning. He did not know about making money. He often went to cut hay② and small trees and sold them to keep himself alive.

He walked along carrying a bundle③ of firewood④ on each end of his shoulder pole, and as he walked he read aloud. His wife followed along behind him, carrying firewood on her back. She tried to persuade⑤ her husband again and again not to read aloud along the way. But Zhu

---

①native adj. 出生(地)的；n. 本地人： He is a native of Beijing. 他是北京人。

②hay n. (作牲口饲料用的)干草

③bundle n. 捆： a bundle of firewood 一捆柴

④firewood n. 木柴,柴火

⑤persuade v.t. 说服,劝服： persuade sb. to do (或into doing) sth. 说服某人做某事

raised ①his voice still louder instead. His wife felt ashamed of him, and sued for a divorce②.

[古文]

薛谭学讴于秦青,未穷① 青之技,自谓尽之,遂辞归。秦青弗止,饯于郊衢,②抚节悲歌,声振林木,响遏行云。薛谭乃谢求反,终身不敢言归。

——《列子·汤问》

[今译]

薛谭向秦青学唱歌,没有学到秦青的全部技巧,就自认为已把老师的本领都学到手了,于是他向老师告辞回家。秦青并不挽留他,在郊外大道上为他饯行。席间,秦青拨动琴弦,悲痛地唱着歌。歌声震荡着树林,树枝随着高亢的歌声轻轻摇摆,树叶簌簌,骄傲地为一代歌手伴奏。歌声直冲云霄,白云停下来,欣赏这动人心弦的歌唱。薛谭感到惭愧,打消了回家的念头,恳求老师把他留下。从此以后,他再也不敢提回家的事了。

---

①穷:穷尽,完全。
②衢:[qú]四通八达的道路。

[英译]

Learning Vocal①Music

Xue Tan had been learning vocal music from Qin Qing, and after a short time he thought he had mastered his teacher's virtuosity② and told his teacher that he was going home. His teacher Qin Qing didn't urge③him to stay.

The farewell party④ took place by the road side not far from the city on the day of Xue's departure⑤. During the dinner, Qin Qing sang a farewell song for his pupil. So accompanied by the melody⑥ of a plucked⑦ instrument, the vocalist⑧ began.

---

①vocal   adj.   声音的：vocal music 声乐
②virtuosity   n.高级演奏术
③urge   v.t. 力劝；力请
④farewell party   饯行宴会
⑤departure   n. 离去
⑥melody   n. 美妙的音乐
⑦pluck   v.t.   拨；弹
⑧vocalist   n. 声乐家,歌唱家

[Oh! What a magnificent song! It was simply a miracle①of vocal music.] The nearby woods were shaken②by his voice, and the branches of the trees rocked③and swayed④on the waves of his song. [The leaves of the trees felt proud⑤because the singing of this wonderful vocalist was accompanied by their rhythmic⑥ rustling⑦] His voice reached the sky where the white clouds paused⑧to enjoy his touching⑨ singing.

Xue Tan who felt ashamed, changed his mind and asked sincerely to continue his study. From that moment on he never asked to go home again.

---

①miracal   n.   奇迹
②shake (shook, shaken) v.t.   摇动
③rock   v.i. 摇摆
④sway   v.i. 摇曳
⑤proud   adj. 骄傲的
⑥rhythmic   adj. 有节奏的
⑦rustling   n. 瑟瑟、沙沙声
⑧pause   v.i. 暂停,中止
⑨ touching adj. 动人的

说话诀窍

[古文]

子禽问曰:"多言有益乎?"墨子曰:"虾蟆蛙蝇,日夜而鸣,舌干擗然① 而不听。今鹤鸡时夜而鸣,天下振动。多言何益?唯其言之时也。"

——《墨子·言语》

[今译]

墨子和他的学生子禽在池塘边散步。子禽问道:"先生,请问多说话有好处吗?"墨子回答:"那要看说什么话。比如池塘里的蛤蟆,无论白天还是夜晚,都是呱呱咕咕地叫个不停。尽管叫得口干舌燥,但因没有意义,也无人理睬。可是,鸡窝里的雄鸡,只在天亮时啼那么两三次,大家知道,鸡啼就要天亮,都很注意。所以,说话不在多少,要看有用还是没用。"

---

① 擗然:指叫声。

The Secret of Talking

The philosopher①Mozi was taking a walk with his pupil Ziqin around a pond②. The pupil asked:

" Master, do people really gain profit③ from talking much?"

Mozi replied:

"That depends on what they talk about. For instance, the frogs in the pond croak④ from morning till night, but who would ever pay attention to their croaking since it has no meaning? The croaking of frogs only annoys us. But what about the crowing⑤ of a rooster? A rooster⑥ crows only a few times at the crack of

---

①philosopher　n. 哲学家;思想家;学者
②pond　n. 池塘
③profit　n. 好处,益处
④croak　v.i. (蛙或鸦)发出的嘎声
⑤crow　v.i. 啼叫
⑥rooster　n. 公鸡,雄鸡

dawn①, yet people pay great attention to its crowing, because they know it means first morning light. Therefore, it is unimportant whether one talks much or little; the key point is that one should speak to a useful purpose."

---

① at the crack of dawn = at the first light of day; at the first morning light 破晓时

婆媳棋局

[古文]

王积薪棋术功成,自谓天下无敌。将游京师,宿于逆旅①。既灭烛,闻主人媪②隔壁呼其妇曰:"良夜难遣,可棋一局乎?"妇曰:"诺。"曰:"第几道下子矣!"妇曰:"第几道下子矣!"各言数十。媪曰:"尔败矣!"妇曰:"伏局。"积薪暗记。明日覆其势,意思皆所不及也。

——李肇 《唐国史补》

[今译]

王积薪下棋技术的功力很深,自以为世上没有敌手。他到京城长安游历,途中在一家旅馆住宿。晚上熄烛就寝以后,听见店主老妇隔着墙壁叫他的媳妇说:"这样美好的夜晚没什么可消遣,能下一盘棋吗?"媳妇说:"行。"老妇说:"我在第几道下一个子了。"媳妇说:"我也在第几道下了一个

---

①逆旅:旅馆,客舍。逆:"迎接"的意思。
②媪(ǎo):年老的妇人。

子了。"双方各自说了几十次。后来老妇说:"你输
了。"媳妇说:"我认输了。"王积薪把这盘棋的着法
暗暗记住,第二天重演婆媳双方攻守的局势,发现
其中的奥妙,都是他所远远不及的。

[英译]

A Game①of Chess Between

Mother-in-law and

Daughter-in-law

Wang Jixin, who was a wizard②at playing
Chinese chess, considered himself unmatched in
the world. When journeying to the capital
(Chang'an), he put up at an inn on the way.
Extinguishing③the candle at night, he went to
bed and subsequently④heard that next door the

---

①game   n.(比赛中)的一局,一盘,一场
②wizard   n.有杰出才干的人
③extinguish   v.t. 熄(灯)
④subsequently   adv. 接着

innkeeper was having a chat with her daughter-in-law in their respective① rooms separated by a partition②.

" What a nice night!" Said the mother-in-law, "What do you think of passing the time by playing a game of chess?"

"All right," the daughter-in-law replied.

" I have placed a chesspiece③ on such and such a line of the chessboard④," called out the old lady.

"And I have placed a piece on such and such a line of the board too," replied the young woman. Both kept on playing by calling out in this way. After some several ten turns, the old lady shouted, "you lost⑤!"

" Yes, I concede ⑥ defeat⑦," replied the young woman.

---

①respective   adj. 各自的,各个的
②partition   n. 隔墙
③chesspiece   n. 棋子
④chessboard   n. 棋盘
⑤lose (lost, lost)   v.i. 输
⑥concede   v.t. 承认
⑦defeat   n. 失败

Wang secretly memorized the moves to this games of chess by heart: The following day when he replayed the offensive①and defensive②moves to that game of chess in the exact same way as the innkeeper and her daughter—in—law had done the previous night, he found every one of their moves to be wonderful and profound, far beyond his own skill.

---

①offensive   adj. 进攻
②defensive   adj. 防御

人 才 篇

The Chapter of Talent

不爱丑恶

[古文]

简子有臣尹绰、赦厥。简子曰："厥爱我，谏我必不于众人中。绰也不爱我，谏我必于众人中。"尹绰曰："厥也，爱君之丑而不爱君之过也；臣爱君之过而不爱君之丑。"

——《说苑·臣术》

[今译]

赵简子有两个助手，一个叫尹绰，一个叫赦厥。一天，赵简子对人说："赦厥是很爱戴我的，他从来不肯在众人面前说我的过错。那个尹绰可不是这样，他总喜欢当着别人的面批评我的缺点，我真受不了。"尹绰听到这话，就去找赵简子，说："赦厥从不留心你的过错，请你改正，因为我不爱你的丑恶。丑恶的东西有什么可爱呢？"

Disliking Ugly Things

Zhao Jianzi had two aids①, one called Yin Chuo and the other, She Jue. One day Zhao Jianzi commented②:

"My aid She Jue, who esteems③ and cherishes④me, never talks about my faults⑤in the presence of others. [But I simply can no longer bear the way my other aid, Yin Chuo,treats me.] He doesn't like me and always criticizes my faults and mistakes in the presence of others.

After hearing it, Yin Chuo went to see Zhao and said:

[" You're wrong about us.] She Jue never pays attention to your faults and mistakes, but cherishes your virtues together with the ugly side

---

①aid n. 助手
②comment v.i. 议论,发表意见
③esteem v.t. 尊敬
④cherish v.t. 珍爱
⑤fault n. 缺点

of your moral①character②. [I often notice your faults and mistakes and ask you to mend③your ways and correct your mistakes.] I don't esteem and cherish what is ugly in you. [What is to be cherished in ugly things?]"

---

①moral adj. 道德的；品行端正的
②character n. 特性；品格
③mend v.t. 改进；纠正，改正： mend one's ways 改过自新

韩信受辱胯下

[古文]

淮阴屠中少年有侮信者,曰:"若虽长大,好带刀剑,中情怯耳。"众辱之曰:"信能死,刺我;不能死,出我胯下!"于是信孰视之,俯出胯下,蒲伏。一市人皆笑信,以为怯。

—— 司马迁　《史记·淮阴侯列传》

[今译]

有一次,在淮阴城里卖肉的少年中间,有一个人瞧不起韩信,当众侮辱他说:"虽然你长得高大,喜欢带着刀剑,其实是个胆小鬼。"

这个少年还当着大家羞辱韩信,说:

"你不怕死,就来刺我;你怕死,就从我的裤裆底下钻过去!"

这时,韩信仔细地打量了对方一番,二话不说,就脸朝地,从那人的胯下爬了过去。

于是,集市上都耻笑韩信,认为他是个胆小鬼。

Going Through Under the

Butcher's①Legs

A youth among the butchers in the city of Huai Yin once spat② at Han Xin, saying:

"Though you are big and tall and like to wear a sword, you are at heart③ a coward④!"

In presence of a large group of spectators⑤, he went on with scorn⑥:

"Look here, Xin, if you are not afraid of death, stab⑦ me; otherwise, crawl through between my legs."

Thereupon, Han Xin, after sizing up the youth carefully, crawed on the ground through

---

①butcher　n. 屠夫
②spit (spat)　v.i. 蔑视,吐唾沫
③at heart = in reality 其实,实际上
④coward　n. 懦夫
⑤spectator　n. 旁观者
⑥scorn　n. 蔑视,耻笑
⑦stab　v.t. 刺

his legs.

The whole town laughed at Xin, thinking him a coward.

孔融少年机智

[古文]

孔文举年十岁,随父到洛。时李元礼有盛名,为司隶校尉。诣门者皆俊才清称及中表亲戚,乃通。文举至门,谓吏曰:"我是李府君亲。"既通,前坐。元礼问曰:"君与仆有何亲?"对曰:"昔先君仲尼与君先人伯阳,有师资之尊,是仆与君奕世为通好也。"元礼及宾客莫不奇之。太中大夫陈韪后至,人以其语语之,韪曰:"小时了了,大未必佳。"文举曰:"想君小时,必当了了。"韪大踧踖。

——刘义庆 《世说新语》

[今译]

孔融(字文举)十岁时,跟着父亲来到洛阳。当时,李膺(字元礼)名声很大,他担任最高检察官。到李府登门拜访的人,都要才学出众、很有声誉或是李府的中表亲戚才通报传达。

孔融到府门前,对门吏说:"我是李府的亲戚。"通报后,进屋坐定。李元礼问他:"你和我是什么亲戚?"

孔融回答:"以前,我的先祖孔仲尼和你的先祖李耳有过称师就学的关系,因此,我家和你家世世代代交情很深啊!"李元礼和在座的宾客对孔融的回答都大为惊讶。

谏议官陈韪后到。有人把孔融的话告诉了他。陈韪说:"小时候聪颖灵敏,长大了不见得就聪明。"孔融接过话头说:"想必你小时候一定是很聪明的了。"陈韪听了,十分局促不安。

[英译]

Kong Rong's Quick Wits in Childhood

When Kong Rong (styled Wenju) went to Luoyang, the then capital, with his father, he was only ten years old. At that time, Li Ying (styled Yuanli), the supreme① offical inspector, was a man of great reputation in the country. Nobody except his relatives and those who possessed

————————

①supreme adj. 最高的

distinct① attainments② and high commen-
dation③ would be admitted to his presence.

"I'm a relative of your master," said the boy
to the gate officer, who at once led him in. Sitting
before the host④, Kong Rong was questioned by
Li Ying:

"What relationship is there between you and
me?"

"In old times, my forefather Confucius had
a teacher-pupil relationship with your
ancestor⑤ Lao Zi (styled Boyang)," replied the
boy guest, "and therefore our two families have
been closely related for many generations." Li
Ying and all his other guests present were greatly
surprised at the answer.

Chen Wei, the counsellor⑥, came later and
was told what Kong Rong had said. " Being
bright in early childhood does not necessarily

---

①distinct adj. 明显的
②attainments n.(常用复数)成就,造诣
③commendation n. 称赞
④host n. 主人: a host country东道国
⑤ancestor n. 祖先
⑥counsellor n. 谏议官;律师

mean that he will be clever when grown up," he observed. In response to this, Kong Rong said, "I guess you must have been very bright in your childhood," which made Chen Wei feel very embarrassed①.

---

①embarrass v.t. 使窘迫

超　迁

[古文]

谊① 年二十余，最为少。每诏令议下，诸老先生未能言，谊尽为之对，人人各如其意所出。诸生于是以为能。

文帝悦之，超迁，岁中至太中大夫②。

——班固　《汉书·贾谊传》

[今译]

贾谊年纪二十出头，是朝臣中最年轻的。每当皇帝诏令臣下议事，老博士们一时答不上来，贾谊却一一为他们作答，人人觉得象是按各自心意来表达的。众博士因此把贾谊看作才能出众的人。

文帝很喜欢贾谊，将他破格提拔，一年之中就让他升到太中大夫。

---

①贾谊：西汉著名的政治家，文学家。
②太中大夫：官名

Speedy Promotion

Jia Yi was the youngest supreme official in the Han imperial court①, for he was then only in his early twenties. Whenever the emperor called in all officials to discuss the affairs of state, if the senior② scholars failed to give a prompt③ answer, Jia could always reply to the emperor's questions one by one in place of them, with answers that expressed exactly what each official had in mind. Therefore Jia was considered as a gifted④ scholar.

The emperor, who liked Jia very much, broke a rule to promote him. Within one year, Jia was elevated⑤ to be a chief consultant⑥.

---

①court n. 朝廷
②senior adj. 年长的;地位较高的
③prompt adj. 迅速的,及时的
④gifted adj. 有才华的,有天赋的
⑤elevate v.t. 提升…的职位
⑥consultant n. 顾问

守卫尽职

[古文]

　　吕元膺为鄂岳都团练使,夜登城,女墙已锁,守陴者曰:"军法,夜不可开。"乃告言中丞自登。守者又曰:"夜中不辨是非,虽中丞亦不可。"元膺乃归,明日擢守陴者为大职。

　　　　　　　　——李肇　《唐国史补》

[今译]

　　吕元膺担任鄂州、岳州的都团练使。有一天晚上,他登上城楼巡视,女墙①已经封锁,守卫女墙的士兵说:" 按军法规定 , 夜间不可开门。" 随从告诉这个士兵说,是御史中丞吕元膺亲自上城巡视。这个士兵听后又说:"黑夜之中分辨不出真假,即使是御史中丞也不能开门。"吕元膺只得返回官邸,第二天就提升这个守卫女墙的士兵担任重要职务。

---

①女墙: 城墙上面有垛口的矮墙

Keeping the Best Guard

Lü Yuanying was a military commander in chief of two prefectures①, E and Yue. Once at night he climbed up onto the city wall to patrol②, but the parapet③(a low wall at the edge of battlements④) had already been locked for the night. A soldier who was standing guard said: "According to the military rules, the parapet is not to be opened at night!"

Then a man in the suite⑤ of the commander told the soldier: "Our commander in chief has come to the city wall to patrol in person!"

On hearing this, the soldier replied: "Excuse me, but at night it is hard to tell between true and false, so even in the case of our commander in chief himself, opening the parapet is still not permitted."

---

①prefecture n. 府;专区
②patrol v.i. 巡逻
③parapet n. 女儿墙
④battlement n. (常用复)城垛
⑤suite n. (一批)随从人员

Commander Lü had no alternative① but to return to his official residence② . The following day Lü promoted③ the soldier guarding the parapet to an important post.

---

①alternative   n. 抉择，取舍
②residence   n. 公馆，住宅: an official residence 官邸
③promote   v.t. 提升

马皇后论宝

[古文]

马后闻得元府库输其货宝至京师,问太祖曰:"得元府库何物?"太祖曰:"宝货耳。"后曰:"元有是宝,何以不能守而失之?盖货财非宝,抑帝王自有宝也。"太祖曰:"皇后之意,朕知之矣,但谓以得贤为宝耳。"后曰:"妾每见人家产业厚则骄生,时命顺则逸生,家国不同,其理无二……但得贤才,朝夕启沃,共保天下,即大宝也。"

——余继登 《典故纪闻》

[今译]

马皇后听说元朝府库里的财宝运到了都城,便问明太祖(朱元璋):"得到元朝府库里的什么财物?"太祖说:"珍宝财物。"皇后说:"元朝有这些财物,为什么无法守护而失掉呢?看来,财物不是珍宝,而皇帝有他自己的珍宝!"太祖说:"皇后的意思,我明白了,是说得到贤人才是得到珍宝。"皇后说:"我常常看到:有的人家产业富足就骄横起来,时运顺利就贪图舒适。居家与治国虽然是两码

— 58 —

事，但它们的道理却是一样的……只要得到贤明而有才干的人，早晚得以开诚忠告，君臣同心保住江山，这才是真正了不起的珍宝！"

[英译]

Queen Ma Commenting

on the Treasures[①]

One day when Queen Ma heard that all of the Yuan Dynasty's treasures had been transferred [from the treasury[②] in Beijing] to the new capital [of Nanjing], she asked Emperor[③] Ming Taizu [Zhu Yuanzhang, the founder of the Ming Dynasty]:

"What did you get from the treasury of the Yuan Dynasty?"

"Precious treasures" was the reply.

"The Yuan Dynasty had a lot of treasures,"

---

① treasure   n. 宝物，宝贝
② treasury   n. 国库
③ emperor   n. 皇帝

said Queen Ma, "I wonder why they were unable to protect them and in the end lost them. Perhaps such treasures are not the real treasures of an emperor."

"Oh, I understand you," replied the Emperor, "You mean that gaining worthy persons is just like obtaining① precious treasures."

Queen Ma said:

"Many times I have watched people become arrogant② and imperious③ when their family became well-off④ and who then seek⑤ ease⑥ and comfort at the opportune⑦ moment. Although a family is different from a country, the reasoning is the same... It seems certain that the most precious treasure that an emperor can obtain is able and virtuous⑧ people as cour-

---

①obtain v.t. 获得
②arrogant adj. 骄傲的
③imperious adj. 专横的
④well-off adj. =rich 富有
⑤seek (sought, sought) v.t. 追求
⑥ease n. 安逸
⑦opportune adj. 合适的,恰好的
⑧virtuous adj. 有品德的,善良的

tiers[1], who are open-minded and always completely sincere in their advice and who work together to protect their country."

---

[1]courtier   n. 臣子

德 性 篇

The Chapter of Morality

恶者贵,美者贱

[古文]

　　阳子之宋,宿于逆旅。逆旅人有妾二人,其一人美,其一人恶,恶者贵而美者贱。阳子问其故,逆旅小子对曰:"其美者自美,吾不知其美也;其恶者自恶,吾不知其恶也。"阳子曰:"弟子识之。行贤而去自贤之行,安往而不爱哉!"

——《庄子·山木》

[今译]

　　有一次,阳子到宋国去,寄宿在一家旅店里。这家旅店主人有两个老婆,其中一个长得很漂亮,另一个长得很丑陋。可是,长得丑陋的却受到店主人的器重,而长得很漂亮的却被店主人瞧不起。阳子问其中原因。旅店主人回答说:"那个长得漂亮的自以为很美,我不知道她美在哪里;那个长得丑的自己以为很丑,我却不觉得她丑。"阳子听了后说:"弟子们记住吧。一个人行为高尚而能去掉自以为高尚的行为,到哪里不受人爱重呢?"

The Ugly①is Noble, the

Beautiful is Base②

Yangzi arrived in the State of Song and put up③at an inn. The innkeeper had two concubines④: one pretty yet contemptible⑤and the other ugly yet respectable. When Yangzi asked him for the reason, the innkeeper replied:

"The pretty one is extremely conscious⑥of her own prettiness, but I don't see any prettiness in her. The ugly one is extremely conscious of her own ugliness, but I don't see any ugliness in her."

"My pupils should remember this well," said Yangzi. "If a person does good deeds but never entertains⑦ any thought of his own virtues, he

---

①ugly adj. 丑陋的；n.丑陋的人(或动物、东西)

②base adj. 贱的,劣的

③put up 住宿;得到食宿

④concubine 小老婆,妾

⑤contemptible adj. 卑鄙的,不齿的,可轻视的

⑥conscious adj. 意识到的,自觉的

⑦entertain v.t. 持有(信心，意见等)；抱着,怀着

will be esteemed① anywhere he goes."

---

① esteem   v.t. 尊敬,尊重

宝 贝

　　宋人或得玉,献诸子罕,子罕弗受。献玉者曰:"以示玉人，玉人以为宝也,故敢献之。"子罕曰:"我以不贪为宝,尔以玉为宝,若以与我,皆丧宝也。不若人有其宝。"

　　　　　　　——《左传·襄公十五年》

[今译]

　　宋国有个人得到了一块玉石,把它献给齐国大夫子罕,子罕不肯收下。献玉石的人说:"我拿它给玉匠看了,他说这是块宝石,所以我才敢把它献给您。"子罕说:"我把不贪财当做宝贝,你把玉石当作宝贝。如果你把玉石给我了,咱俩都失掉了自己的宝贝呵! 还不如各自都保留自己的宝贝吧。"

The Treasure

One day a man from the State of Song procured① a piece of jade and offered it to Zihan, [a minister from the State of Qi], who, however, refused② to accept the gift.

The flatterer③ said:

"I have shown this precious stone to a jade master who regarded ④ it as a very valuable object; thus I dare to offer it to you."

Zihan replied:

"You consider this jade a treasure, but my treasure is to refuse bribes⑤. If you give the jade to me, both of us lose something precious. So let us keep our respective treasures to ourselves."

---

①procure   v.t. (设法)获得,(努力)取得
②refuse   v.t. 拒绝
③flatterer   n. 奉承的人
④regard...as   把…认为是
⑤bribe   n. 贿赂

大公无私

晋平公问祁黄羊曰:"南阳无令,其谁可而为之?"祁黄羊对曰,"解狐可。"平公曰:"解狐非子之仇邪?"对曰:"君问可,非问臣之仇也。"平公曰:"善。"遂用之,国人称善焉。居有间,平公又问祁黄羊曰:"国无尉,其谁可为之?"对曰:"午也可。"平公曰:"午非予之子邪?"对曰:"君问可,非问臣之子也。"平公曰:"善。"又遂用之,国人称善焉。孔子闻之曰:"善哉,祁黄羊之论也,外举不避仇,内举不避子,祁黄羊可谓公矣。"

——《吕氏春秋》

[今译]

有一天,晋平公问祁黄羊:"南阳县缺个县长,你看派谁去当合适?"祁黄羊说:"叫解狐去最合适了。"平公惊奇地问:"解狐不是你的仇人吗?你为什么要推荐他呢?"祁黄羊:"你只问我派谁去合适,并没有问我,解狐是不是我的仇人啊!"平公说:"你说得对。"解狐当南阳县的县长,替老百姓办了许多好事,大家都称赞他。过了一些日子,平公又问祁黄羊:"现在朝廷里缺个法官,你看谁能胜任?"祁黄羊回答:"祁午是能够胜任的。"平公又惊奇起来了,问道:"祁午不是你的儿子吗?"祁黄羊说:"你只问我谁能胜任,并没问我,祁午是不是我的儿子啊!"平公说:"你说得对。"祁午当法官,替老百姓办了许多好事,受到大家称赞。孔子听到这两件事,说:"祁黄羊说得真好啊!他推荐人,完全拿才和德做标准,不因为是自己的仇人,存了偏见,便不推荐他;也不因为是自己的儿子,怕人议论,而不推荐他。象祁黄羊这样的人,才算得上'大公无私'啊!"

[英译]

Most Selfless

One day Marquis Ping of Jin said to Qi Huangyang: "The need for a magistrate ① in the county of Nanyang has arrisen. Whom do you consider fit for the post?"

"Xie Hu is", relied Qi Huangyang.

---

①magistrate　n. 地方行政官: the county magistrate 县长

"Is not Xie Hu your personal enemy? Why do you recommend him as the magistrate?"

"You asked me who is fit for the post, not whether Xie Hu is my personal enemy, didn't you?"

"That's right," said Marquis Ping who subsequently approved① of the selection.

Xie Hu was indeed a good magistrate of Nanyang County, and the people praised him.

After some days, the Marquis asked Qi Huangyang once again: "The need for a judge② of the high court has been felt. Whom do you think fit for the post?"

"Qi Wu is," answered Qi Huangyang. "Is not Qi Wu your son?"

"You asked me who is fit for the post, not whether Qi Wu is my son, right?"

"Right you are!" agreed Marquis Ping.

Qi Wu, who turned out to be a good judge, was praised highly by the people.

---

①approve v.i. 赞成,认可
②judge n. 法官

On hearing this, Confucius remarked[①]: "What Qi Huangyang said is marvellous[②]. He recommended a person according to his ability and moral character. He didn't refuse to recommend his personal enemy or his own son, which shows he was not blinded by prejudice[③] or constrained[④] by street gossip[⑤]. Qi Huangyang is most selfless."

---

① remark v.t. 谈论,评论
② marvellous adj. 极妙的,了不起的
③ prejudice n. 偏见,成见: have a prejudice against (in favour of) sb. 对某人有偏见(偏爱)
④ constrain v.t. 强迫: constrain sb. **to do** sth. 强制某人做某事
⑤ gossip n. 流言蜚言: be fond of gossip 喜欢说人闲话

匈奴不灭,无以家为

[古文]

去病为人少言不泄,有气敢往。

上尝欲教之吴、孙兵法,对曰:"顾方略何如耳,不至学古兵法。"

上为治第①,令视之,对曰:"匈奴不灭,无以家为也。"由此上益爱重之。

—— 班固 《汉书·霍去病传》

[今译]

霍去病沉默寡言,不轻易发表意见,但他有胆气,敢勇往直前。

汉武帝曾想教他学吴起、孙子的兵书,霍去病说:"看实际情形考虑用什么样的策略罢了,不必完全按照古代兵书。"

汉武帝为他建造府第,叫他去看看,霍去病说:"匈奴不消灭,哪里要什么家啊。"从此,武帝就更加喜爱、看重他了。

————————

①第:官僚和贵族的大住它。

How Dare I Make My Home

Before Wiping Out① the

Xiongnu Enemy?

[Huo Qubing was a famous general of the Han Dynasty.] He was a person of few words who did not express his opinions rashly②. Still, he was courageous③ and dared to advance bravely.

Emperor Han Wudi once told him to study the authoritative books on military skills written by Wu Qi and Sun Zi, but Huo said: "Let us make tactical④ decisions during a campaign⑤ according to each situation as it happens. It is unnecessary to act totally under the instructions from ancient books."

---

①wipe out 消灭
②rash adj. 轻率的; rashly adv.
③courageous adj. 勇敢的
④tactical adj. 策略的
⑤campaign n. 战役

The Emperor had a new house built especially for Huo Qubing, and told him to go and have a look at it. He replied: "How dare I make my home before wiping out the Xiongnu enemy?" From that moment on, the Emperor liked and respected him all the more.

大树将军

[古文]

　　异为人谦退不伐①,行与诸将相逢,辄引车避道。进止皆有表识,军中号为整齐,每所止舍,诸将并坐论功,异常独屏树下,军中号曰:"大树将军。"

　　　　——范晔　《后汉书·冯异传》

[今译]

　　冯异为人谦虚,从不自夸。外出与其他将领相逢时,就转车让路。他的部队进退行止都有明确号令,在汉军中以整齐闻名。每当宿营,众将坐在一起争功,冯异经常退避到树下,军中称他为"大树将军"。

---

①伐：夸耀

[英译]

"Tall—Tree General"

General Feng Yi was always modest, and never cared to boast① about himself. Each time he ordered his driver to steer② toward the roadside in order to yield the way to the vehicles of his fellow generals who passed by.

Feng's troops, in advancing and retreating③, at all times followed his clear and definite commands, and were famous for keeping their ranks④ in perfect order in Han Dynasty Army.

Taking up quarters⑤,the generals used to sit together, quarreling over their own merits⑥, while General Feng took a rest under a tall tree without saying anything. Thus he became known in the army as the "Tall—Tree General."

---

①boast   v.i. 吹嘘

②steer   v.t. 驾驶

③retreat   v.i. 后退

④rank   n. (军)行列;(复)队伍;军队;士兵

⑤quarters   n. 住处;(军)营房: take up quarters 宿营

⑥merit   n. 功绩,功劳;(有时用复)功过,功罪

天知,神知,我知,子知

[古文]

　　杨震为东莱太守,当之郡,道经昌邑。故所举荆州茂才王密为昌邑令,谒见。至夜怀金十斤以遗震。震曰:"故人知君,君不知故人,何也?"密曰:"暮夜无知者。"震曰:"天知,神知,我知,子知。何谓无知!"密愧而出。

——范晔　《后汉书·杨震列传》

[今译]

　　杨震任东莱郡太守,上任时,路过昌邑县,从前他所荐举的荆州秀才王密在这里做县令。王密拜见了他,入夜带了十斤黄金赠送杨震。杨震说:"老朋友了解你,你不了解老朋友,这是什么道理呢?"王密说:"夜间没有人知道(我赠金给你)。"杨震说:"天知道,神知道,我知道,你知道,怎么说没有人知道!"王密羞愧地走了出去。

No Absolute①Secret

Yang Zhen, having been appointed as the prefect② of Donglai, started out for the prefectural seat. On the way he came to Changyi County③. Wang Mi, a *xiucai* * from Jingzhou, whom Yang Zhen had appointed as magistrate④of this locality⑤, called to pay him respects. When night fell, Wang came again, this time to offer him a gift of 160 taels⑥ of gold.

"We've been friends for a long time. I know you well, and so should you know me well," said Yang Zhen. "What's all this for?"

"Never mind. In the dark hours no one will have any knowledge of this."

"Heaven knows, the spirits know, you know

①absolute   adj. 绝对的
②prefect   n. 长官: prefectural seat 长官的职位
③county   n. 县;郡
④magistrate   n. 地方行政官: the county magistrate 县长
⑤locality   n. 地方,所在地
⑥tael   n. 银两(中国古代货币单位)

and I know. What do you mean by no one will know?"

Wang felt ashamed and withdrew①.

* One who passed the imperial civil examination at the county level.

---

①withdraw (withdrew, withdrawn) v.i. 离开；退出

以此遗之，不亦厚乎

[古文]

（杨震）……后转涿郡太守。性公廉，不受私谒①。子孙常蔬食步行，故旧长者或欲令为开产业，震不肯，曰："使后世称为清白吏子孙，以此遗之，不亦厚乎！"

——范晔　《后汉书·杨震列传》

[今译]

杨震改任为涿郡太守。他正直廉洁，不接受私人的拜会请托。子孙们每日素食步行。杨震的老友长辈中有人要他为儿孙们置些财产，杨震不愿这样做，说："我让后人称他们是清官的子孙，把这品德留给他们；这'财产'不也很厚重吗！"

---

①谒：拜见

To Bequeath① Them with Morality②, Is That Not Also Precious?

Yang Zhen assumed③ a new official post as the prefect of Zhuo. He was honest and upright, refusing those persons who asked him to help arrange something or who sought④ good offices. His sons and grandsons were brought up to obstain⑤ from eating meat and to go on foot. Some of his old friends and seniors suggested that he should purchase⑥ durable wealth for the sake of his descendants⑦, but Yang Zhen was unwilling to do so, saying:

---

①bequeath　v.t.　遗赠
②morality　n.　道德,美德,德行,品行
③assume　v.t.　担任
④seek (sought)　v.t.　追求;寻找
⑤abstain　v.t.　戒
⑥purchase　v.t.　购买
⑦descendant　n.　子孙,后裔

"Let later generations praise them, for they are the worthy descendant of an honest and upright official. Is not such 'morality' which I bequeath them with just as precious as wealth?"

糟糠之妻不下堂

[古文]

帝姐湖阳公主新寡,帝与共论朝臣,微①观其意。主曰:"宋公威容德器,群臣莫及。"帝曰:"方且图之。"

后弘被引见,帝令主坐屏风后,因谓弘曰:"谚言贵易交,富易妻,人情乎?"弘曰:"臣闻贫贱之知不可忘,糟糠之妻不下堂②。"

帝顾谓主曰:"事不谐③矣。"

——范晔《后汉书·宋弘列传》

[今译]

光武帝的姐姐湖阳公主新近守寡,光武帝跟她谈论朝廷大臣,悄悄地观察她的心意。湖阳公主说:"宋弘容貌威严德才兼备,大臣们没有比得上他的。"光武帝说:"我将替你考虑这件事。"

---

①微: 暗暗地、悄悄地
②下堂: 旧谓妻子被丈夫休退或和丈夫离异。
③谐: 调合的意思。

后来宋弘受到光武帝接见,光武帝叫公主坐在屏风后面,就对宋弘说:"俗话说,地位高了就要更换朋友, 富裕了就要另娶妻子, 这是人之常情吗?"宋弘说:"我听说贫贱时的知心朋友是不能忘记的,患难与共的妻子是不可遗弃的。"

光武帝回头对公主说:"事情办不成了。"

[英译]

A First Wife in Poverty① Should

Not be Forsaken②

Emperor Guangwu's sister, princess Huyang was newly widowed③. Once the Emperor discussed with her the officials in the imperial court, and when doing so, carefully observed her intentions.

"The supreme official Song Hong is digni-

---

①poverty　n. 贫困
②forsake (forsook, forsaken)　v.t. 遗弃
③widow　v.t. 使成寡妇

fied① in appearance," said the princess, " and
has both ability and political integrity②. No official in the court can be compared with him."

"I'll try to find a way," said the Emperor.

Later Song Hong was called for an interview
with the Emperor, who meanwhile had ordered
the princess to sit behind a screen and said:

" As the saying goes: 'A man who rises in
status③ will trade his old friends for new friends;
if he is well—off④,he will trade his old wife for a
new wife.' It is the natural and normal thing for
people to do, isn't it?"

" Your Majesty," replied Song, " I have
heard of another saying:' A faithful friend in
poverty should not be forgotten; a wife who en-
dured hardship and woe⑤ by one's side should
not be forsaken.'"

Then the Emperor turned his head back and

---

①dignify   v.t. 使尊贵，使有威严
②integrity   n. 正直
③status   n. 地位,身份
④well—off   adj. 富裕
⑤woe   n. 悲痛

said to the princess behind the screen: "We failed to find a way!"

爱 莲 说

[古文]

　　水陆草木之花,可爱者甚蕃。晋陶渊明独爱菊。自李唐来,世人甚爱牡丹。予独爱莲之出淤泥而不染,濯清涟而不妖,中通外直,不蔓不枝,香远溢清,亭亭净植,可远观而不可亵玩焉。予谓菊,花之隐逸者也;牡丹,花之富贵者也;莲,花之君子者也。噫! 菊之爱,陶后鲜有闻;莲之爱,同予者何人?牡丹之爱,直乎众矣!

——宋·周敦颐

[今译]

　　水中和陆地各种草木所开的花,可爱的很多。晋朝诗人陶渊明唯独喜爱菊花。自从唐朝以来,世上的人们非常喜爱牡丹。可是,我却独爱莲花,因为它虽然扎根在污泥里,但不被污泥所染;它虽然沐浴在清彻的池水中,但不显媚态。它的躯干内通外直,没有枝蔓,越在远处越能闻到它发出的清香。它皎洁纯净,挺拔直立,只可供人们在远处观赏,却不可近前玩弄。我认为:菊花是隐逸之花,牡丹是富贵之花,莲花是君子之花。唉!我很少

听到陶渊明之后还有谁喜爱菊花?也不知道还有
谁跟我同样喜爱莲花?不过,我想喜爱牡丹的人,当
然是很多的了!

[英译]

Ode① to the Lotus②

There are a lot of lovely flowers among the
various herbaceous③, woody, aquatic④ and ter-
restrial⑤ flora. The poet Tao Yuanming of the
Jin Dynasty liked only the chrysanthemum⑥.
Since the Tang Dynasty, the peony⑦ has been
loved passionately⑧ by the people at large. My
sole love is the lotus: it grows up from out of the

---

①ode n. 颂歌,颂诗
②lotus n. 莲花
③herbaceous adj. 草本的
④aquatic adj. 水生的
⑤terrestrial adj. 陆地的: terrestrial flora 陆地植物
⑥chrysanthemum n. 菊花
⑦peony n. 牡丹
⑧passionate adj. 热情的; passionately adv.

mire① yet avoids being contaminated② ; it bathes itself in the clean, clear water and yet does not look coquettish③; its stem④ is hollow⑤ and straight; it never trails⑥ or branches⑦; its pure scent⑧ spreads far away; it stands upright in water with moonlight purity. It can be enjoyed by looking at it from a distance only and cannot be approached and touched indecently⑨.

Such is my opinion: among flowers, chrysanthemum is of the hermit⑩; peony is of the rich and honoured; lotus is of the noble. Alas! I've hardly heard of anyone who liked chrysanthemums so much after Tao Yuanming; I don't know who holds the same love for the lotus as I; but surely, the peony is loved by the many.

---

①mire   n. 沼地,泥泞,泥土
②contaminated   a. 污染,沾污
③coquettish   adj. 卖弄风情的
④stem   n. 茎
⑤hollow   adj. 中空的
⑥trail   v.i. 蔓延
⑦branch   v.i. 长出枝子,分叉,分枝
⑧scent   n. 香味
⑨indecently   adv. 粗鲁地
⑩hermit   n. 隐士

教 化 篇

The Chapter of Teaching

曾子教子

[古文]

　　曾子之妻之市,其子随之而泣,其母曰:"女还,顾①反为女杀彘。"妻适②市来,曾子欲捕彘杀之,妻止之曰:"特与婴儿戏耳。"曾子曰:"婴儿非与戏也。婴儿非有知也,待父母而学者也,听父母之教,今子欺之,是教子欺也。母欺子,子而不信其母,非所以成教也。"遂烹彘也。

　　　　　　　　　——《韩非子·外储说左上》

[今译]

　　曾子的妻子到市上去,她的儿子哭闹着要跟着她去。曾子的妻子说:"你回去,等我回来时,杀猪给你吃。"妻子从市上回来,曾子要捉猪杀给儿子吃,妻子叫他不要杀,说:"这不过是和孩子说着玩的。"曾子说:"小孩子不可以和他说着玩。他们没有知识,全学父母的样子,听父母的言谈。现在你欺骗他,不是教他欺骗吗? 母亲欺骗儿子,儿子

①顾: 回头看
②适: 到……地方去。

不相信母亲，这不是教养之道。"于是杀猪烧给儿子吃。

[英译]

Zengzi Teaching His Son

When Zengzi's wife was ready to go to the market, her son cried and begged to go with her.

"No, you stay at home, my dear," she said. "After I return home, I will kill a pig and cook① it for you."

After she returned home from the market, Zengzi wanted to catch the pig and butcher② it. His wife did not want him to kill the pig.

"I was only kidding③ with the child," she told him.

"We must be serious with children," replied

---

① cook v.t. 煮，烧，烹调： cook-book 食谱,烹调书
② butcher v.t. 屠宰
③ kid v.i. 开玩笑： I am not kidding. 我讲这话不是开玩笑的。

Zengzi. "They learn from their parents' example and listen to what their parents say. If we try to cheat① them, it means we are teaching them to deceive people. If a mother dupes② her son, finally the son will not believe her. That is not a good way to teach children". Therefore, Zengzi killed the pig and cooked it for his son.

---

①cheat   v.t. 欺骗
②dupe   v.t. 欺骗,诈骗: dupe sb. into doing sth. 骗某人去做某事

为父浣洒

建老白首,万石君尚无恙。

每五日洗沐,归谒亲,入子舍,窃问侍者,取亲中裙厕①牏②,身自浣③洒,复与侍者,不敢令万石君知之,以为常。

——班固 《汉书·万石君传》

石建年迈发白时,他的父亲万石君(即"石奋")还健在。

石建每逢五天一次假日,就回家探望父亲,到了自己房里,便悄悄向侍者了解父亲的近况,从侧门(悄悄)拿来父亲的内衣,亲自洗涤干净,再交给侍者,还不敢让父亲知道,认为这是日常必做的事。

---

①厕:通"侧"
②牏(yú):通"窬",此是指门。
③浣:洗涤

Washing Father's Underclothes[①]

Personally[②]

[Shi Jian was a senior official in the Han Dynasty.] When he himself was old with white hairs, his father, Shi Fen, was still living and enjoyed good health. Shi Jian had a holiday every five days and on that day he returned home to see his father.

Entering his own room, he always quietly asked the servant about how things were with his father. Then he took his father's underclothes secretly from the side door and washed them clean. When they were dry, he gave them back to the servant. He did not let his father know because he thought that this was simply his duty.

---

①underclothes　n. 衬衣,内衣,贴身衣
②personally　adv. 亲自

李存审戒子

[古文]

存审出于寒微,常戒诸子曰:"尔父少提一剑去乡里,四十年间,位极将相,其间出万死获一生者非一,破骨出镞①者凡百余。"因授以所生镞,命藏之,曰:"尔曹生于膏粱②,当知尔父起家如此也。"

——司马光 《资治通鉴》

[今译]

李存审出身于门第卑微的家庭,经常告诫儿子们说:"你们的父亲年轻时带着一口剑离开家乡,四十年来,官做到将相,中间不止一次历万死才获一生的险境,剖开骨头取出的箭头就有一百多个。"接着他把所取出的箭头给了儿子们,嘱咐他们好好收藏着,说:"你们生长在富贵之家,应当知道你们的父亲就是这样起家的啊!"

---

①镞:箭头。
②膏粱:指富贵之家。

General Li Cunshen's Advice

to His Sons

The General Li Cunshen, who was descended① from a humble② family, often gave advice to his sons, saying:

"When I was young, I left home with a sword. In a space of forty years I won promotion③ from an officer to a general, during which many a time④ I narrowly escaped from death. More than one hundred arrowheads were taken out from between my bones."

Then he showed his sons the arrowheads, and told them to store them well. He then said:

"All of you were born into a rich and honoured family. But you should know how your

---

①descend v.i. 下降,出自： be descended from an ancient
   family 是一个古老家族的后裔
②humble adj. 地位低下的
③promotion n. 提升
④many a time 多次,常常

father built himself and this family up from diffi-culties and hardships."

惠 子 善 譬

[古文]

客谓梁王曰:"惠子之言事也,善譬①。王使无譬,则不能言矣。"王曰:"诺。"明日见,谓惠子曰:"望先生言事则直言耳,无譬也。"惠子曰:"今有于此而不知弹者,曰:'弹之状何若?'应曰:'弹之状如弹'。谕乎?"王曰:"未谕②也。"于是更应曰:"'弹之状如弓,而以竹为弦',则知乎?"王曰:"可知矣。"惠子曰:"夫说者固以其所知,喻其所不知,而使人知之。今王曰无譬,则不可矣。"王曰:"善。"

——刘向 《说苑》

[今译]

有人在梁王面前嘲笑惠子:"这个惠子,说话爱用比喻,假使不准他用比喻,他一定什么也说不明白了。"梁王说:"哦。"第二天,梁王接见惠子,就对他说:"你以后讲话,就直截了当地说,不要再用

---

① 譬:比喻。
② 谕:明白

比喻了。"惠子说:"现在有个人,不知道'弹'是什么样的一种东西。你告诉他,'弹'就是'弹',他听得明白吗?"梁王说:"那怎么能明白呢!"惠子说:"如果我告诉他,弹的形状象弓,弦是用竹子做的,是一种射箭工具,我这样说,他能明白吗?"梁王说:"可以明白了。"惠子说:"用别人所已经了解的,来比喻他还不了解的,目的是要使他了解。你让我说话不用比喻,那怎么行呢?"梁王说:"你说得对呀!"

[英译]

Making Good Use of
Metaphors① and Analogies②

A certain person ridiculed③ Huizi to the King of Liang: "Huizi can speak only in metaphors and analogies. If Your Majesty were to forbid him to use them, he wouldn't be able to

---

①metaphor n. 隐喻(一种修辞手段)
②analogy n. 类似,相似
③ridicule v.t. 嘲笑,嘲弄;奚落

say anything clearly." The King agreed.

The next day the King of Liang gave an interview to Huizi and told him: "From now on please talk plainly, speak straight to the point and don't use metaphors and analogies anymore."

Huizi said: " If someone tells me that he doesn't know what is meant by *dan*, and I tell him a *dan* is a *dan*, do you think he will understand?"

"Of course he won't," replied the King of Liang.

"Well, suppose I explain that a *dan* resembles① a bow in shape, that its string② is made of bamboo, and that a *dan* is used in archery③. Do you think he'd understand?"

"Yes, I think he would."

"I employ④ that which is already understood by people in metaphors and analogies to

---

①resemble　v.t. 象,类似
②string　n. 线,细绳,带子
③archery　n. 射箭
④employ　v.t. 使用,雇用

explain to people what they do not yet understand," said Huizi. "How could I stop using metaphors and analogies as you have ordered me?"

With this, the King of Liang replied: "You are quite right!"

教学相长

[古文]

　　虽有嘉肴,弗食,不知其旨也;虽有至道,弗学,不知其善也。是故学,然后知不足;教,然后知困。知不足, 然后能自反也, 知困, 然后能自强也。故曰, 教学相长也。

—— 《礼记》

[今译]

　　即使有了美味佳肴,却不去品尝,就体会不到它的可口。即使有了完善的学说,却不去学习,就体会不到它的优越性。可见,只有投入于学习,才了解自己的欠缺;只有从事于教人,才了解困难所在。由于了解自己的欠缺,才能自我反省;由于了解困难所在,才能坚持不懈地克服困难,因此,教和学是相辅相成的。

To Teach is to Learn

Even when there is good food, you will not know its deliciousness① if you don't taste② it; even when there is a good doctrine③, you will not know its virtue if you don't learn it. Therefore, to learn makes us realize our deficiency④, and to teach makes us know the difficulties.

Having realized our deficiency, we may then come to reflect⑤; having known the difficulties, we may be able to strengthen⑥ ourselves to overcome⑦ them. So we say, to teach is to learn.

---

①delicious   adj. 芬芳的,美味的,可口的
②taste   v.t. 尝味
③doctrine   n. 学说
④deficiency   n. 不足,欠缺
⑤reflect   v.i. 反省(on, upon),思考
⑥strengthen   v.t. 加强
⑦overcome (overcame, overcome)   v.t. 克服

三　友

益者三友,损者三友。友直,友谅,友多闻,益矣。友便辟①,友善柔②,友便佞③,损矣。

——《论语·季氏篇》

[今译]

有益的朋友有三种,有害的朋友也有三种。同正直的人交朋友,同诚实的人交朋友,同见识广博的人交朋友,这是有益的。同惯于走歪门邪道的人交朋友,同善于阿谀奉承的人交朋友,同惯于花言巧语的人交朋友,这是有害的。

---

①辟: 邪僻
②柔: 与"刚"相对,此指阿谀奉承。
③佞(nìng):惯于用花言巧语谄媚人。

Three Kinds of Friends

It will be helpful to make friends with three kinds of poeple —— those who are upright, those who are trustworthy①, and those who are knowledgeable②.

It will be harmful to make friends with another three —— those who do evil③, those who engage in flattery④, and those who are used to saying sweet words.

---

①trustworthy adj. 值得信任的,可靠的
②knowledgeable adj. 有知识的,渊博的
③evil n. 邪恶,罪恶
④flattery n. 奉承,捧场,谄媚的举动

三 戒

[古文]

　　君子有三戒:少之时,血气未定,戒之在色;及其壮也,血气方刚,戒之在斗;及其老也,血气既衰,戒之在得。

——《论语·季氏篇》

[今译]

　　君子有三件事情要警惕:年轻时,血气还不成熟,要警惕贪恋女色;到了壮年时期,血气正旺,要警惕好胜喜斗;到了老年时期,血气已经衰退,要警惕贪得无厌。

[英译]

Three Exhortations①

A gentleman ought to avoid three things.

---

①exhortation　n. 告戒

When in youth, with sap① in growth, avoid lust②; when in the prime③ of life, with vigour④ in full, avoid bandying⑤; when in old age, with vitality⑥ in decline, avoid greed⑦.

---

①sap　n. 元气,活力
②lust　n. 色欲,淫欲
③prime　n. 青春: in the prime of life 在壮年时期
④vigour　n. 活力,精力: with vigour in full / full of vigour 血气方刚,朝气蓬勃
⑤bandy　v.t. 把…打来打去
⑥vitality　n. 生命力: with vitality in decline 血气衰弱
⑦greed　n. (for) 贪心

三　乐

[古文]

　　益者三乐,损者三乐。乐节礼乐,乐道人之善,乐多贤友,益矣。乐骄① 乐,乐佚② 游,乐宴乐,损矣。

——《论语·季氏篇》

[今译]

　　有益的喜好有三种,有害的喜好也有三种。喜好以礼乐节制自己,喜好说别人的长处,喜好多交贤德的朋友,这是有益的。喜好靡靡之音,喜好游手好闲,喜好大吃大喝,这是有害的。

————————

①骄: 放纵。
②佚(yì): 同"逸"。安乐;安闲。

Three Delights①

There are three beneficial delights and three harmful delights. The former include the delights of self—restraint② by following the proprieties③ and rites④, of acclaiming⑤ others' virtues, and of multiplying⑥ worthy friends; while the latter consist of the delights of enjoying decadent⑦ music, of going in for wanton⑧ pleasure, and of indulging⑨ in sumptuous feast-ing⑩.

N.B. There was a translator who rendered the latter part like this: "… to enjoy oneself in false pride, in sauntering and in feasting."

---

①delight   n. 快乐，乐趣
②self—restraint   n. 克己
③propriety   n. 礼节
④rite   n. 仪式
⑤acclaim   v.t. 赞扬
⑥multiply   v.t. 增加
⑦decadent   adj. 颓废的
⑧wanton   adj. 放肆的
⑨indulge   v.i. 放任
⑩sumptuous feasting   奢侈宴会

习 惯 说

[古文]

蓉少时,读书养晦堂之西偏一室。俯而读,仰而思;思而弗得,辄起,绕室一旋。室有洼径尺,浸淫①日广;每履之,足苦踬②焉;既久而遂安之。一日,父来室中,顾而笑曰:"一室之不治,何以天下国家为?"命童子取土平之。后蓉复履其地,蹴然③以惊,如土忽隆起者;俯视之,坦然则既平矣。已而复然,又久而后安之。噫!习之中人甚矣哉!

——清 刘 蓉

[今译]

刘蓉少年时期,在养晦堂西边小屋里用功。有时,他埋头读书;有时,他抬头思考。当他思考再三,对问题仍不理解时,就站起身来,在室内来回走动。室内泥地有个坑,直径大约一尺。随着时光

———————

①浸淫:连续不断。
②踬(zhì):被绊倒。
③蹴然:吃惊的样子。

的流逝,坑愈来愈大了。他每次走过坑地,常常绊跌。但时间一长,他对坑也就感到习惯了。一天,父亲走进他的书房,看到坑地,笑着说:"一个小小的房间尚且弄不整齐,将来怎能为国家效劳呢?"于是,父亲叫书童用土把坑填平。起初,刘蓉走在它上面,很吃惊,似乎觉得这块泥地隆起了。他低头一看,才知这块泥地已填得平平坦坦。这样过了一段时期,他才对这块平地感到习惯成自然了。唉,习惯对人的影响是多么巨大啊!

[英译]

On Habit

When Liu Rong was young, he studied in a western room of the Cultivating① Obscurity② House. Sometimes he bent down to read; sometimes he looked up to think. When he could not, after much thinking, understand the meaning of what he was reading, he rose to his feet and walked about the room. In the earthen

---

①cultivate   v.t. 培养,磨练
②obscurity   n. 暗淡,朦胧,不引人注目,偏僻

floor of the room there was a hollow about one foot wide which grew larger day by day. Every time he walked over it, he stumbled①; but by degrees, he got used to it.

One day his father came into his study. Seeing the hollow in the floor, his father said smilingly, "How can you serve your country well, when you cannot even keep such a little room tidy②?" His father ordered a servant to fill it up with earth. Later when Liu walked over the spot③ again, he was surprised to find that the floor there seemed to swell④. He looked down and found the hollow had been filled up and the ground was now as flat as a pancake⑤. It took some time before he could get used to it again. Ah! How habit works on⑥man!

---

①stumble　v.i. 绊跌,绊倒
②tidy　adj. 整齐的
③spot　n. 地点,场所
④swell　v.i. 变大,膨胀
⑤as flat as a pancake　象薄煎饼一样扁平
⑥work on　影响

哲 理 篇

The Chapter of Philosophy

学无所用

[古文]

　　鲁人身善织屦①,妻善织缟②,而欲徙于越。或谓之曰:"子必穷矣。"鲁人曰:"何也?"曰:"屦为履之也,而越人跣③行,缟为冠之也,而越人被发。以子之所长,游于不用之国,欲使无穷,其可得乎?"

——刘向　《说苑》

[今译]

　　有个鲁国人专长做鞋,他的妻子专长织绢。夫妻俩打算迁到越国去。有人对他们说:

　　"如果迁居到越国去,你们必然变得穷困了。"

　　"那为什么呢?"那个鲁国人问。

　　对方回答:"谁都知道,制鞋是为了穿在脚上的,但越国人都赤脚行走。织绢是为了制作帽子的,但越国人留长发不戴帽子。现在你们身怀这

---

①屦(jù):古时用麻葛等制成的鞋。
②缟:未经染色的绢。
③跣(xiǎn):赤脚。

种专长,到一个对你们的专长一无用处的国家去,怎能不变得穷困呢?"

[英译]

Your Skills Are Useless

A man of the State of Lu was good at making hempen① shoes and his wife at weaving② gauze③. They intended④ to move to the State of Yue. They were told that they would become poor if they should do so.

"Why do you think so?" asked the husband.

Some people told him:

"Everybody knows shoes are made for the feet, but the people of Yue go barefooted; Gauze is used for making hats, but the people of Yue go bareheaded. Now you are going with your special skills⑤ to a country where they are

_____

①hempen   adj. 大麻制的
②weave (wove, woven)   v.t. 织
③gauze   n. 素色绢
④intend   v.t. 打算
⑤skill   n. 技巧,技能

useless. How can it be that you will not become poor?"

世无良猫

[古文]

　　某恶鼠,破家求良猫。餍① 以腥膏②,眠以毡
罽 ③。猫既饱且安,率不捕鼠,甚者与鼠游戏,鼠以
故益暴。某怒,遂不复蓄④ 猫,以为天下无良猫
也。

——乐钧　《耳食录》

[今译]

　　有一个人很讨厌老鼠,花费了很多钱财,买到
一只好猫。他用鲜美的鱼肉喂它,让它睡在毛毯
上。猫吃得又好又饱,而且生活过得很安逸,就不
抓老鼠了,甚至还和老鼠一起游戏,老鼠因此闹得
更凶了。这人非常生气,于是再也不养猫了,以为
世界上没有好猫。

----

①餍(yàn): 饱,吃饱。
②膏: 脂肪
③罽(jì): 一种毛织品。
④蓄: 蓄养

There Is Not A Single Good

Cat in the World

Once upon a time there was a man who hated mice, so he spent a lot of money on a good cat. He fed① it delicious② fish and let it sleep on a rug③.

The cat was so well fed and lived such a comfortable life of leisure④ that it played with mice instead of⑤ catching them. As a result, the mice made more noise and caused more trouble. The man became furious⑥ with the cat and finally got rid of⑦ it. From then on, he would not keep another cat as he thought that there was

---

①feed (fed, fed)　v.t. 喂(养)

②delicious　adj. 美味的

③rug　n. 小地毯

④leisure　n. 悠闲,安逸

⑤instead of 代替,而不: I have come instead of my brother. He is ill. 我来顶替我的兄弟,他病了。

⑥furious　adj. 暴怒

⑦to get rid of　摆脱; 本文中作"不再养"解。

not a single good cat in the world.

瞎子摸象

[古文]

有王告大臣,汝牵一象来示盲者,时众盲各以手触。大王唤众盲问之,汝见象类何物?触其牙者言象形如萝菔根。触其耳者言如箕,触其脚者言如臼。触其脊者言如床。触其腹者言如瓮,触其尾者言如绳。……

——《涅盘经》

[今译]

从前,有位国王告诉他的大臣:牵一头象来给盲人看。盲人各用手去摸象。国王再把那些盲人叫来问道:"你们说说,象是什么样子?"摸了象牙的,就说象如同萝卜根一样;摸着了象耳的,就说象如同簸箕一样;摸着了象脚的,就说象同舂米的臼一样;摸着了象脊背的,就说象好比一张床;摸着了象肚皮的,就说象好比大瓮坛一样;摸着了象尾巴的,就说象好比一条绳子。……

The Blind Touching An Elephant

One day a King said to his ministers: "Bring an elephant here and show it to the blind."

After the blind touched it with their hands, the King asked:

"Now, each of you tell me what an elephant is like?"

"Your Majesty! It seems like a radish① root," replied the first blind person, who had grasped one of its tusks②.

"My Lord! It is just like a dustpan③," answered the second one, who had touched its ear.

The third one, who happened to take hold of one of its feet, said it was very much like a ram④.

---

①radish   n. 小萝卜
②tusk   n. (象、猪等的)长牙
③dustpan   n. 畚箕
④ram   n. 夯;压头;撞锤

The fourth one, who had put his hands on its back, said it was something like a bed.

The fifth one, who had touched its belly①, said it was no more than a big earthen jar②.

The sixth one, who had caught hold of its tail, said it was nothing but a rope.

[Everybody took a one—sided approach③ to the elephant.]

---

①belly n. 肚,腹部
②jar n. 罐子,坛子
③approach n. 接近;看法

晏子使楚

[古文]

晏子将使楚。楚王闻之……"欲辱之"……晏子至,楚王赐晏子酒。酒酣,吏二人缚一人诣王。王曰:"缚者曷为者也?"对曰:"齐人也,坐盗。"王视晏子曰:"齐人固善盗乎?"晏子避席对曰:"婴闻之,橘生淮南则为橘,生于淮北则为枳,叶徒相似,其实味不同,所以然者何?水土异也。今民生于齐不盗,入楚则盗,得无楚之水土使民善盗耶?"……

——《晏子春秋》

[今译]

齐国的晏子,出使到楚国去。楚王听说晏子来当大使,有意要当着晏子的面侮辱齐国。一天,楚王摆了酒席,招待晏子。正当他们吃得高兴时,有两个小官绑着一个犯人来见楚王。楚王故意问道:"这人犯了什么罪?"小官回答说:"他是一个强盗! 他是齐国人。"楚王回头对晏子说:"原来齐国人是惯于当强盗的。"晏子站起来答道:"大王,我听说生长在淮南的橘树,移植到淮北,就会变成枳树。从外表上看,橘和枳的叶子是一样的,但这两种果子的味道却完全不同。我们齐国的老百姓从来不做强盗,一到楚国就干起犯罪的勾当来,我看,这也许是水土的关系吧。"……

[英译]

The Ambassador[①] to the State of Chu

Yanzi of the State of Qi was appointed as the Ambassador to the State of Chu. On hearing it, the King of Chu decided to insult[②] the State of Qi in Yanzi's presence.

One day, the King of Chu invited Yanzi to a banquet[③]. At the height of the entertainment two petty[④] officials led in a convict[⑤] bound[⑥] with

---

①ambassador　n. 大使
②insult　v.t. 侮辱
③banquet　n. 宴会,盛宴
④petty　adj. 下级的,地位低微的
⑤convict　n. 罪犯
⑥bind (bound) v.t. 捆,绑

rope.

"What crime has he committed?" asked the King of Chu on purpose.

"He's a robber! He's from the State of Qi."

The King of Chu turned round and said to Yanzi: "I didn't expect the people of Qi to be hardened① bandits②."

Getting up from his table, Yanzi replied: "Your Majesty! I've heard that the orange trees which grow on the southern bank of the river Huai become trifoliate③ when transplanted④ to the northern bank of the Huai. Though the two sorts of trees look the same, their fruits taste quite different from each other. People in our state never engage in robbery⑤ but only begin to commit crimes once they are in the State of Chu. Would you say this is due to the change in environment⑥?"

---

①harden   v.t. 使变得冷酷,使麻木

②bandit   n. 土匪,盗匪

③trifoliate   adj. (植)具三小叶的

④transplant   v.t. 移植

⑤robbery   n. 抢劫,盗取

⑥environment   n. 环境

比　美

[古文]

　　邹忌……朝服衣冠，窥镜，谓其妻曰："我孰与城北徐公美？"其妻曰："君美甚。徐公何能及君也！"城北徐公，齐国之美丽者也。忌不自信，而复问其妾曰："吾孰与徐公美？"妾曰："徐公何能及君也！"旦日，客从外来，与坐谈，问之客曰："吾与徐公孰美？"客曰："徐公不若君之美也。"明日，徐公来，熟视之，自以为不如；窥镜而自视，又弗如远甚。暮寝而思之，曰："吾妻之美我者，私我也；妾之美我者，畏我也；客之美我者，欲有求于我也。"

—— 《战国策》

[今译]

　　一天，邹忌早晨起来，穿戴好衣帽，照着镜子问他的妻子："我同城北徐公比，哪一个漂亮？"他的妻子答："你漂亮多啦！徐公怎能跟你比？"城北徐公是齐国的美男子。邹忌自己有点不相信，再去问他的妾："我同城北徐公比，谁更美？"妾说："徐公哪里比得上你美！"次日，有个客人从外边来访。邹忌同他坐下聊天,就问他:"我同徐公比,哪一个美?"客人答:"徐公比不上你美!"第二天,徐公来访。邹忌仔细地把徐公打量了一番,自己觉得比不上徐公;再对着镜子照照自己,更觉得自己确实比不上徐公。夜里,他躺在床上想了又想,才恍然大悟:"我妻子偏爱我,所以吹捧我美,我的妾惧怕我,所以奉承我美;客人上门有求于我,所以故意讨好我。"

[英译]

Who Is Better-looking

Early one morning, after dressing himself in front of a mirror①, Zou Ji asked his wife:

"Who is better-looking, Xu Gong from the north of the city or I?"

"Certainly, you are much better-looking," answered his wife, "How can Xu Gong possibly be compared with ② you!"

Now, Xu Gong was famous in the State of

---

①mirror　n. 镜子
②(be) compared with　与…相比

Qi for his attractive① appearance, and Zou Ji could hardly believe what his wife said. So he inquired of his concubine:

"Who is more handsome, Xu or I?"

" How can Xu Gong be compared with you!" replied his concubine.

The next day, a guest dropped in②, and while having a chat③ with him Zou Ji asked the same question.

"You are more handsome than Xu Gong," said the guest.

The next day Xu Gong called on④ Zou Ji, who scrutinized⑤ Xu and found Xu really more handsome than himself. He stole a glance at himself in the mirror⑥ and realized that he couldn't be compared with this handsome Xu Gong.

After going to bed that night, Zou Ji thought deeply for a long time and finally

---

①attractive　adj. 诱人的,有吸引力的
②drop in (on)　偶然来访
③have a chat　聊天,闲谈
④call on　访问,拜访
⑤scrutinize　v.t.　细察,详审
⑥steal a glance at sb. in the mirror　在镜中偷看某人

understood the truth. His wife had praised① him because she loved him; his concubine had flattered② him because she feared him; and the guest had fawned③ on him because he wanted a favour.

---

①praise   v.t. 称赞
②flatter   v.t. 奉承
③fawn v.i.(on, upon)   巴结,奉承

窃 鸡 贼

[古文]

有控窃鸡者某，令唤左右邻讯之，均不认，环跪案下，佯①为不理，另审别案。久之，又佯作倦容曰："汝等且回去。"众皆起。令忽勃然拍案大叫曰："窃鸡贼亦敢起去耶？"其人不觉，悚②然屈膝，一讯而服。

——魏息园 《不用刑审判书》

[今译]

有人控告鸡被偷了。县令把他的左右邻居唤来讯问，大家都不承认偷鸡。被讯问的人围绕公案跪在下面。县令假装不予理睬，另外审理别的案子。时间久了，县令故作疲倦的样子，懒洋洋地说："你们暂且回去吧。"众人都站了起来，以为没事了，刚想离去，县令突然发怒，拍案大喝一声："偷鸡贼也敢离去吗？"偷鸡人没有精神准备，心惊胆

①佯：假装
②悚：恐惧。

怯,屈膝跪倒,一经审讯,就服了罪。

[英译]

The Hen Thief①

When a man accused② that his hen had been stolen, the county magistrate summoned all the neighbours to his presence to investigate it. Every one of them denied③ having stolen it, and knelt down before the magistrate in the court.

The county magistrate pretended not to ask further about the case. He went on trying other cases. In the course of time④, he put on an appearance of being tired, saying: "You folks⑤ go home for the time being."

On hearing this, everybody stood up, [thinking that they were free to go.] Hardly had they begun to leave, when the county magistrate sud-

---

①thief n. 贼
②accuse v.t. (of) 控告
③deny v.t. 否认
④in the course of time = when enough time has passed
⑤folks n. infml. 人们

denly became very angry, and striking his desk, shouted: "How dare the hen thief leave this court?"

The thief wasn't prepared for it, and was so awfully frightened that he knelt down again. No sooner had the thief been interrogated① than he admitted that he had stolen the hen.

---

①interrogate v.t. 审问，审讯，讯问

天下无马

[古文]

马之千里者,一食或尽粟一石。食马者不知其能千里而食也。是马也,虽有千里之能,食不饱,力不足,才美不外见,且欲与常马等不可得,安求其能千里也!策之不以其道,食之不能尽其材,鸣之而不能通其意,执策而临之曰:"天下无马!"呜呼!其真无马邪!其真不知马也!

——韩愈 《昌黎先生集》

[今译]

日行千里的马,每顿要吃一石多粮食。养马的人不知道它日行千里需要吃这么多的粮食。这种马,虽然具有日行千里的能力,但吃不饱,力气不足,它的才能就表现不出来,而且连一匹普通的马也比不上,哪能要求它日行千里呢!赶它奔驰,又很不得法;喂它,又不让它尽量吃饱;吆喝它,又不懂它的癖性,养马的人拿起马鞭走到马前说:"世界上没有好马!"呜呼!真的没有好马吗?这真是不识好马啊!

There Is Not a Single

Good Horse in the World

A horse able to run one thousand li in a day must eat a *dan*① (one hectolitre②) of grain③ at a feeding. The groom④ who feeds it does not know it needs to eat this much in order to run that fast. So even though the horse may have the ability to gallop⑤ a thousand miles, if underfed⑥, it will lose its strength and be unable to demonstrate⑦ its splendid⑧ capability⑨.

---

①*dan* n. 石（10斗）Chinese system，折合公制100升，折合英制 2.7497 浦式耳

②hectolitre n. 公石

③grain n. 粮食

④groom n. 马夫

⑤gallop v.t. 驰行

⑥underfed adj. 吃得太少的

⑦demonstrate v.t. 演示

⑧splendid adj. 完美的，绝妙的

⑨capability n. 能力

Moreover it will not be able to be compared with even a common horse, let alone be expected to fulfil① its natural speed!

A master treats his horse most unreasonably: he rides it haphazardly②, he feeds it but without letting it have its fill, he urges it loudly while failing to understand its natural proclivity③. And, then he comes down upon his horse with a whip④, saying that there is not a single good horse in the world.

Alas! Is it true what he says? Or rather is it because he himself has no knowledge whatsoever of horses?

---

①fulfil v.i.(-ll-) 完成
②haphazardly adv. 任意的,无计划的
③proclivity n. 癖性,脾气
④whip n. 马鞭

不禁火,民安作

[古文]

　　成都民物丰盛,邑① 宇② 逼侧,旧制禁民夜作,以防火灾,而更相隐蔽,烧者日属。

　　范乃毁削先令,但严使储水而已。百姓为便,乃歌之曰:"廉叔度,来何暮? 不禁火,民安作。……"

　　　　　——范晔　《后汉书·廉范传》

[今译]

　　成都地方民富物丰,可是民房毗连狭窄。原先规定禁止百姓夜间干活,以防止火灾。然而人们更是偷偷地点灯夜作,火灾也就接连不断。

　　廉范上任后, 就取消了旧的禁令,只是严格规定每家储水罢了。百姓感到很方便,就歌颂道:"廉叔度, 为什么来得那么迟? 你不禁止点灯,我们安心劳作。……"

---

①邑: 城
②宇: 房檐

People Working at

Night with Lamps

[In the Han Dynasty,] people were well-to-do① and products abundant② in the city of Chengdu. Only the houses were adjoined③ too closely. At first, people were forbidden④ to work at night in order to protect the houses from fire. However, they worked more secretly with lamps at night, and fires broke out ⑤ one after another.

[After Lian Fan, the new prefect, assumed⑥ office,] he cancelled⑦ the former or-

---

①well-to-do　adj. 经济宽裕
②abundant　adj. 丰富的,充裕的
③adjoin　v.t. 毗连,毗邻
④forbid (forbade / forbad, -bidden)　v.t. 禁止
⑤break out　(突然)发生
⑥assume　v.t. 担任, 承担: assume office 就职
⑦cancel　v.t. 取消

der, but strictly stipulated① that water had to be reserved for every house in case of fire. People considered it to be very convenient for themselves, and praised him: "Why didn't you come earlier, our Prefect Lian? You never forbid us to light lamps, so we can work at our ease at night..."

---

① stipulate   v.t. 规定

三世廷尉

[古文]

雄少时家贫。丧母,营① 人所不封② 土者,择葬其中。丧事趣办,不问时日。巫皆言当族灭,而雄不顾。

及子诉孙恭,三世廷尉③,为法名家。

——范晔 《后汉书·郭躬列传》

[今译]

吴雄年轻时家境贫穷。母亲去世,吴雄就在他人不愿筑坟的地方,选了块墓地葬在那里。丧事立即就办,不选择日子。搞巫术的都说,这样做会家破人亡,可是吴雄不理睬。

后来,吴雄连同他的儿子吴诉、孙子吴恭,三代都做了廷尉,成为法律专家。

---

①营:建造。
②封:埋葬。
③廷尉:掌管刑法的最高法官。

Three Generations on the Chair

of the Supreme① Law Court

Wu Xiong was descended from a poor family. When his mother died, he chose a site which his fellow people considered to be unfit as a burial ground, and had her corpse② buried there.

The funeral service was carried out immediately without caring whether the date of burial would lead to good or bad luck. The witches③ foretold④ the forthcoming⑤ misfortunes that the whole family with all of its members would die without any descendants. Those Wu never minded.

Afterwards Wu Xiong was appointed to the chair of the supreme law court, and his son Wu

---

①supreme　adj. 最高的
②corpse　n. 死尸,尸体
③witch　n. 巫;女巫
④foretell (foretold)　v.t. 预言
⑤forthcoming　adj. 即将到来的

Xin and grandson Wu Gong later also held the same post, so Wu's family had the post of authority in the law court for three successive[①] generations.

---

①successive   adj. 相继的，连续的

令反侧子自安

[古文]

　　四月，进围邯郸，连战破之。五月甲辰，拔其城，诛王郎。

　　收文书，得吏人与郎交关谤① 毁者数千章。

　　光武不省，会诸将军烧之，曰："令反侧子自安。"

　　——范晔　《后汉书·光武帝纪》

[今译]

　　公元24年农历4月，(刘秀)围攻邯郸，一连几仗挫败了王郎军队。5月27日，刘秀攻克邯郸，杀了王郎。

　　接收王郎宫中文书档案时，查获官吏私通王郎。毁谤刘秀的书信几千件。

　　刘秀看也不看，会集众将当场烧掉，说："让那些三心二意的人安下心来。"

―――――――

①谤：公开指责别人的过失。

Let the Half–hearted

Personnel① Feel at Ease

In April of the year 24 A.D. by the luner calendar, General Liu Xiu besieged② the city of Handan and after waging③ a series of campaigns④, defeated⑤ Wang Lang's army. On May 27, Liu Xiu captured⑥ the city and executed⑦ his enemy Wang Lang.

When taking over the written documents, they discovered thousands of personal communications⑧ to Wang Lang from various officials which slandered⑨ Liu Xiu. Liu, however, without ever reading through them, burnt all of them

---

① personnel n. [集合名词]全体人员
② besiege v.t. 围攻
③ wage v.t. 发起,发动
④ campaign n. 战役
⑤ defeat v.t. 打败
⑥ capture v.t. 占领
⑦ execute v.t. 将…处死
⑧ communication n. 书信,通报
⑨ slander v.t. 诽谤

in the presence of his men, saying, " Let the half—hearted personnel feel at ease!"

赵括之母

[古文]

……秦攻赵,孝成王使括代廉颇为将。将行,括母上书言于王曰:"括不可使将。"王曰:"何以?"曰:"始妾事其父,父时为将,身所奉饭者以十数,所友者以百数;大王及宗室所赐币帛,尽以与军吏、士大夫;受命之日,不问家事。今括一旦为将,东向而朝军吏,吏无敢仰视之者;王所赐金帛,归尽藏之;乃日视便利田宅可买者。王以为若其乎?父子不同,执心各异。愿勿遣!"王曰:"母置之,吾计已决矣。"括母曰:"王终遣之,即有不称,妾得无随乎?"王曰:"不也。"括既行,代廉颇三十余日,赵兵果败,括死军覆。王以母先言,故卒不加诛。

——刘向 《列女传》

[今译]

……秦国出兵攻打赵国,孝成王让赵括代替廉颇作将军。将要出发的时候,赵括的母亲向赵王上书说:"不能让赵括做将领。"赵王问:"为什么?"赵括的母亲回答说:"我从前侍奉他的父亲,那时他父亲正做将军。亲自供养的有几十人,以朋友相待的有几百人。国君及王室贵族赠送的钱币绸帛之类的礼物全部拿来送给军中的将领、士大夫。从接受命令那天开始,就不再过问家中的事情了。现在赵括一旦当了将军,面向东坐下,让下属拜见,军下属没有敢抬头看他的。国君赏赐的金银绸缎等财物,都拿回来藏在家里,不给下属。却每天寻找可买的合宜的土地房屋。大王,您认为赵括象他的父亲吗?他们父子思想行事都不一样。希望您不要派遣赵括为将。"赵王说:"你这做母亲的算了吧!我已经决定了。"赵括的母亲说:"大王一定要派他去,如果赵括不能称将军之职,打了败仗,我能不跟着受处罚吗?"赵王说:"不会的。"赵括奉命出发,代替廉颇做将军,仅三十多天时间,赵国军队果然被打得大败,赵括战死,全军覆没。赵王由于赵括的母亲已经有言在先,所以最终没有治她的罪。

Zhao Kuo's Mother

When the State of Qin attacked① the State of Zhao, King Xiaocheng of Zhao appointed Zhao Kuo to replace Lian Po as general. Lian Po had much experience in warfare. Upon Zhao Kuo's setting out, his mother personally went to see the King and said: " Zhao Kuo isn't qualified② as a general."

"Why?" asked the King.

"I used to serve his father who was a general at that time. He provided support for several tens of men, and treated hundreds as friends. He shared all the money and silks which were given to him as gifts by Your Majesty and other noblemen with both his officers and officials. From the day he accepted his appointment on, he didn't pay any attention to his family. Now his son, Zhao Kuo, having been appointed as general, sits facing east and while in-

---

① attack v.t. 进攻，攻击
② qualified adj. 合格的，胜任的

terviewing① his officers, lifts up his horns② so none of them dare to look up at him. He stored all the gold, silver, and silk which Your Majesty gave to him in his house instead of sharing them with his men. Moreover, everyday he is busy with buying suitable land and houses. Your Majesty, what do you think about Zhao Kuo? The father and the son are quite different in both their thoughts and behaviour. I hope you won't appoint Zhao Kuo as general."

"As his mother, you don't have to worry about that," replied the King, "I have made my decision."

"As Your Majesty has done so, were he not qualified or were he defeated, could I be excused③ from punishment?" asked Zhao Kuo's mother.

"Certainly," answered the King.

Instead of the experienced general Lian Po,

---

①interview v.t. 接见
②horn (牛、羊、鹿等动物的)角: lift up one's horns 趾高气
　扬；盛气凌人
③excuse (from) v.t. 给…免去

Zhao Kuo started for the front. It took just over thirty days for Zhao's whole army to come to a complete defeat. Even General Zhao Kuo himself was killed and his whole army was ruined①. Owing to her prophecy②, the King took Zhao Kuo's mother as guiltless③ in the end.

---

①ruin v.t. 使毁灭,使覆灭
②prophecy n. 预言
③guiltless adj. 无罪的

子产知奸

[古文]

郑子产晨出，过东匠之宫，闻妇人之哭也，抚其仆之手而听之。有间，使吏执①而问之；手杀其夫者也。翌②日，其仆问曰："夫子何以知之？"子产曰："其声不恸③。凡人于其所亲爱也，知病而忧，临死而惧，已死而哀。今哭夫已死，不哀而惧，是以知其有奸也。"

——王充　《论衡·韩非》

[今译]

有一次，郑国大夫子产清晨外出，路过东边的一个手艺人家门口时，听到一个女人正在哭。他握住仆人的手，很仔细地听了一会儿。过了没多久，他派一个小官去把那个女人抓来了。经过审问，原来她亲手毒死了自己的丈夫。第二天，

---

①执：捉拿，拘捕
②翌(yì)：明(天，年)
③恸(tòng)：极度悲伤。

仆人问子产:"您怎么知道这个女人的问题呢?"子产回答说:"她的哭声不悲痛。一般人对于自己的亲人,知道他病了,一定很担忧;亲人病危,他一定很恐惧;等到亲人死了,他就会非常悲哀。这个女人哭她的丈夫,哭声并不悲哀,却充满了恐惧,因此,我知道她一定与别的男人有奸情而谋杀了亲夫。"

[英译]
Zi Chan Realizing the Adultery①

One day Zi Chan [a senior② official in the state of Zheng]went out in the early morning. When passing the craftsman's③ house to the east, he heard a woman crying. He held on to his servant's hand and listened carefully for a while.

Very soon he ordered a petty officer to arrest her. After an interrogation④, it turned

---

①adultery n. 通奸
②senior adj. 权位较高的
③craftsman n. 工匠,技工
④interrogation n. 审问

out① that the woman had poisoned her husband with her own hand.

The next day the servant asked Zi Chan: "How did you know what had happened, sir?"

"Her cry wasn't sorrowful②," answered Zi Chan. "Everybody always worries about their relatives if they are laid up③, and certainly fears④ for them if they fall critically⑤ ill, and is terribly sad were they to die. But that woman was crying for her husband with fright not grief⑥. Therefore, I realized her adultery had caused her to poison her husband."

---

①turn out 证明是,结果是,实际情况是
②sorrowful adj. 悲哀的
③lay up (usu. pass.)卧病在床
④fear v.i. (for) 害怕
⑤critically adv. 沉重的,岌岌可危的
⑥grief n. 悲伤

假药误人

[古文]

余病……谒^①医视之。曰:"惟伏神为宜。"明日,买诸市,烹而饵之,病加甚。召医而尤其故,医求观其滓。曰:"吁!尽老芋也。彼鬻^②药者欺子而获售^③。子之懵^④也,而反尤于余,不以过乎?"

——柳宗元 《柳河东集》

[今译]

柳宗元有次生病,请来一位医生给他诊治。医生说:"只有服食上等茯苓最相宜。"第二天,柳宗元派人去市集买了药来,熬了服下去。结果病情反而加重了。再请医生来,追问原因,医生要求查看一下药渣,然后叹口气说:"唉!不是茯

---

①谒(yè): 请求。
②鬻(yù): 卖
③售: 卖出去。
④懵(měng): 无知,糊涂。

苓，尽是些加过工、染过色的老山芋干儿呵。那个卖药的骗人，把假药卖给了你，你无知反而追究医生的责任，不感到惭愧吗?"

[英译]

The False①Medicinal Herbs②Harming Patients

Liu Zongyuan fell ill and a doctor was sent for③.

"Please take some *fuling*④ of the highest quality that you can find," said the doctor.

On the following day, a servant bought the medicinal herbs from the market and concocted⑤ a brew⑥ which he gave to Liu Zongyuan. After taking the medicine, Liu got

---

①false adj. 假的

②herb n. 药草

③send for (a doctor) 派人去请(医生)

④*fuling* (poris cocos) n. 茯苓

⑤concoct v.t. 调制(汤、饮料)

⑥brew n. (酿造出来的)饮料

worse. So he sent for the doctor again and called him to account①.

The doctor, having taken a look at the concocted herbs; heaved② a sigh and said:

[This is not *fuling* at all.] It's just taro③[that has been processed and dyed.] "The medicinal herb seller is a swindler④ and the patient can't tell true medicinal herbs from⑤ false ones and says the doctor is to blame for⑥the mistake instead. Doesn't such a patient feel ashamed?"

---

①call...to account 要求…说明理由,责问,申斥
②heave a sigh 发出一声叹息
③taro   n. 芋头
④swindler   n. 骗子
⑤tell...from 辨别,把…和…区分开
⑥to blame for 对…应负责任,对…该受责备

智 愚 篇

The Chapter of Wit

姜从何生

[古文]

　　楚人有生而不识姜①者，曰："此从树上结成。"或曰："从土里生成。"其人固执己见，曰："请与子以十人为质，以所乘驴为赌。"已而遍问十人，皆曰："土里出也。"其人哑然失色，曰："驴则付汝，姜还树生。"

——江盈科　《雪涛小说》

[今译]

　　楚国有个人，有生以来没有见过生姜，他说："姜是长在树上的。"别人告诉他："姜是在土里生长成的。"这个人却固执己见，说："你去找十个人来问问，我敢以自己骑的毛驴与你打赌。"随后他们就问了十个人，都说："姜是从土里长出来的。"这个人哑口无言，变了脸色，却仍坚持道："毛驴尽管输给你了，但是生姜还是树上长出来的。"

---

①姜：一种植物，栽于壤土或粘土。

Where Does Ginger①Grow?

In the State of Chu there lived a man who had never seen ginger in his life, and he said: "Ginger is found on trees." When he was told: "Ginger certainly grows in the earth," the man strongly stuck② to his own opinion, saying: "Please ask ten other persons about it and I bet③ you the donkey which I ride on that I'm right."

Then they did so, but the reply of these ten people was the same: "Ginger grows in the earth." Even though he was left without an argument④ and had lost all the color in his face, the man persisted in his idea, saying:

"Although I lost my donkey in the bet, ginger still grows on trees."

---

①ginger n. 生姜
②stick(stuck) v.i. (to) 坚持
③bet (bet / betted) v.t. 用(钱或物)打赌
④argument n. 争论,辩论

长 生 术

[古文]

　　昔人有言能得长生者，道士闻而欲学之。比往，言者死矣。道士高蹋①而恨②。夫所欲学，学不死也。其人已死而犹恨之，是不知所以为学也。

——孔鲋　《孔丛子》

[今译]

　　从前传说有人得到长生不死的法术。有个道士听了，就想去学。到了那里，那个会法术的人已经死了。道士捶胸跺脚，遗憾自己来迟了。道士想学的是长生不死的法术，可那个会法术的人连自己的性命也保不住，他还怨恨自己来迟了，这是不知道为什么而学啊!

---

①蹋：顿足。
②恨：遗憾，不满意。

The Magic Art① of Longevity

Once upon a time it was said that there lived someone who had mastered the magic art of longevity②. A Taoist heard this and was determined to go to this person and learn this art. Unfortunately the man of magic arts died before his arrival.

"What a pity! Why did I have to get here so late?" He beat his breast and stamped his feet③ in remorse④.

This Taoist had come all this way for the magic arts. If that master couldn't even keep himself alive with his magic arts, what use would it be to the Taoist? The Taoist was indeed blind as to the use of learning it.

---

①magic art 魔术的技艺
②longevity n. 长寿
③beat one's breast and stamp one's feet 捶胸顿足
④remorse n. 悔恨

曹冲称象

[古文]

曹冲生五、六岁，智意所及，有若成人之智。时孙权曾致巨象，太祖欲知其斤重，访之群下，咸莫能出其理。冲曰："置象大船之上，而刻其水痕所至，称物以载之，则校可知。"太祖悦，即施行焉。

——陈寿 《三国志》

[今译]

曹冲在五、六岁时，智慧和见识已经达到成人的程度。当时孙权曾送给曹操一头大象，曹操想知道大象重多少，询问他手下的臣子，谁都想不出称象的办法来。曹冲说："把大象牵到船上，再把水淹没的痕迹刻下记号，然后装上过了秤的东西，让水再淹没到装大象的痕迹那里，就可以量出大象的重量了。"曹操听了很高兴，就按照上述办法称出了大象的重量。

Cao Chong Weighing

an Elephant

When Cao Chong was about five or six years old, he was so clever that his wit and wisdom① were almost the same as an adult's②. Once Sun Quan sent a big elephant as a gift to Cao Cao, who wanted to know its weight. Cao Cao asked all his men, but none of them could find a way to measure it. At last Cao Chong said:

"Put the elephant in a boat and make a mark of the water level on the side of the boat. Then load the boat with measured goods until it reaches the mark made for the elephant. In this way we will be able to measure out its weight."

Cao Cao was pleased to hear it and ordered his men to do it accordingly③. Before long he got

---

①wisdom　n. 智慧,才智
②aduit　n. 成年人
③accordingly　adv: 照着(办、做)

the weight of the elephant.

误抄祭文

[古文]

东家丧妻母，往祭，托馆① 师撰文，乃按古本误抄祭② 妻父者与之。识者看出，主人大怪馆师，馆师曰："古本上是刊定的，如何会错?只怕是你家错死了人!"

——方飞鸿 《广谈助》

[今译]

东家死了岳母，准备前往祭奠，托私塾老师撰写祭文，塾师就按照古本误抄了一篇悼念岳父的祭文给他。祭奠时，有位懂行的人指出了这个错处，主人责怪塾师，塾师却说："古本上的祭文是刊定的，怎么会错呢? 只怕是你家错死了人吧!"

---

①馆：此指私塾学堂。
②祭：追悼死者。此指悼念的文章。

Copying the Wrong

Funeral① Oration②

When a host was going to attend the funeral ceremony for his mother-in-law who had just died, he asked a teacher in an old-style private school to compose a funeral oration.

From ancient books the teacher copied down one for a father-in-law instead of for a mother-in-law by mistake.

During the funeral ceremony③ a gentleman who knew the ropes④ pointed out the mistake, whereupon the host accused the teacher of mistaking the father-in-law for the mothr-in-law. But the teacher replied:

"The funeral oration from the ancient book was officially⑤ printed and published. How

---

①funeral　n. 丧葬
②oration n. 演说：a funeral oration 悼词,祭文
③ceremony　n. 典礼,仪式,礼节
④know the ropes　知道事情的内情(或窍门、做法、规则等)
⑤officially　adv. 官方地,正式地

could it be mistaken? I'm afraid there must have been a mistake in the death in your family."

刻舟求剑

[古文]

楚人有涉江者，其剑自舟中坠于水，遽① 契其舟，曰："是吾剑之所从坠。"舟止，从其所契者入水求之。舟已行矣，而剑不行，求剑若此，不亦惑乎？

—— 《吕氏春秋·察今》

[今译]

从前，有个楚国人乘舟过江。船到江心时，一不小心，他的佩剑掉进了江里。他急忙在船边刻上一个记号，口里喃喃自语："我的剑是从这儿掉下去的。"最后，当船在对岸停靠下来后，他从做了记号的地方跳进浅水中，去找他的剑。当然，他只是白费功夫。船已经走了很远了，剑却一直沉在掉下去的地方没动，他哪里还能摸到剑呢？思想僵化常常使人变得愚昧不堪。

①遽(jù)：急忙.

Marking the Boat for

the Lost Sword①

Once a man of Chu was crossing a river in a boat. When reaching the middle of the river, his sword dropped into the water because of his carelessness. He quickly cut a mark on the side of the boat and murmured② to himself: "This is where my sword slipped down."

When the boat finally arrived at the other bank, the man of Chu got down into the shallow③ water under the marked place and tried to search for his sword.

[Of course, as you can imagine, his search was useless] for the boat had sailed quite some distance while the sword remained at the same spot④ all the time. A rigid⑤ way of thinking

---

①sword n. 剑,刀
②murmur v.i. 低声说
③shallow adj. 浅的
④spot n. 地点,场所
⑤rigid adj. 僵硬的,刻板的

often makes one a fool.

牧童评画

[古文]

　　蜀中有杜处士①，好书画，所宝以百数。有戴嵩牛一轴，尤所爱，锦囊玉轴，常以自随。一日曝②书画，有一牧童见之，拊掌大笑曰："此画牛斗也。牛斗力在角，尾搐两股间。今乃掉尾，谬矣。"处士笑然之。

　　　　　　　　——苏轼　《东坡志林》

[今译]

　　四川有个隐居的读书人姓杜，十分爱好书画。他珍藏的字画有几百幅，其中有戴嵩画的一幅牛，尤其珍爱。他用彩绸缝成套子，用玉装饰卷轴，经常把它带在身边。有一天，他正在晒书画，来了个放牛娃，看了戴嵩的这幅画，拍掌大笑说："这幅画是画牛斗架的样子。可是，牛打架时，力气都用在牛角上，尾巴搐缩在大腿之间。

―――――――――

①处士：古时称有才德而隐居的人。

②曝（pù）：晒。

这张画上却摇着尾巴，错了。"杜处士听后，笑了笑，认为很对。

A Cowboy Commenting

on the Painting

There was a hermit① scholar in Sichuan whose name was Du. Being fond of the art of calligraphy② and painting, he had hundreds of masterpieces③ in his collection. Out of them all he cherished④ most was a painting of bulls by Dai Song, and so he had it mounted on a jade scroll⑤ roller⑥ and wrapped in a silken⑦ bag to be carried with him all the time.

---

①hermit   n. 隐士
②calligraphy   n. 书法
③masterpiece (=master-work)   n. 杰作,名作
④cherish   v.t. 爱护,珍爱
⑤scroll   n. (羊皮纸)卷轴,纸卷,画卷
⑥roller   n. 滚筒,滚轴
⑦silken   adj. 丝制的,柔软的,光泽的

One day as he was sunning his collection, a cowboy came round. After a glance at Dai Song's picture, he clapped his hands and burst into laughter:

"The painter certainly meant it to be fighting bulls," commented the boy. "While fighting, bulls put all their strength into their horns① and draw their tails② tight③ between their thighs④. But this painting shows their tails wagging⑤. That is a mistake."

The hermit scholar, convinced⑥, gave a smile and nodded⑦.

---

①horn n. 牛角
②tail n. 尾巴
③tight adj. 紧的,拉紧的,绷紧的
④thigh n. 股,大腿
⑤wag v.i. 摇动，摆动
⑥convince v.t. 确信,信服,使认识错误(或罪行)
⑦nod (nodded) v.i. 点头(表示同意或打招呼等)

智匠喻皓

[古文]

　　钱氏据两浙时，于杭州梵天寺建一木塔。方两三级，钱帅登之，患其塔动。匠师云："未布瓦，上轻，故如此。"乃以瓦布之，而动如动。无可奈何，密使其妻见喻皓之妻，赂以金钗，问塔动之因。皓笑曰："此易耳，但逐层布板讫，便实钉之，则不动矣。"匠师如其言，塔遂定。盖钉板上下弥束，六幕联如胠① 箧②，人履其板，六幕相持，自不能动。人皆伏其精练。

——沈括 《梦溪笔谈》

[今译]

　　钱氏任浙东浙西两省省长时，下令在杭州梵天寺造一座木塔，该造第三层时，钱氏登上塔，发现塔动，很担心。匠师说："还没铺瓦，因上部轻，所以塔动。"等到铺好全部瓦片，但塔动依

---

①胠(qū)：通"阹"，围,拦。
②箧(qiè)：小箱子。

然。匠师一筹莫展，暗中叫他的老婆去见喻皓的妻子，赠送金钗，请教塔动的原因。喻皓笑一笑说："这很容易，只要每层间加上支杆用铁钉固定，塔就不动了。"匠师按照喻皓的指教去做，木塔屹立不动了。原因是上下左右前后六面用钉子固定支杆，紧密联接，如同箱子。人走在支杆上，由于杆件相互支持，塔就稳固不动了。大家对喻皓这种技术上的指教表示钦佩。

[英译]

A Wise Architect①

The governor② of the provinces of East and West Zhejiang, Mr. Qian, ordered that a wooden pagoda③ be built at the Brahma−Heaven Temple in Hangzhou. When the third floor of the building was to be completed, he went up to the top floor to inspect④ the work. He found it

---

①architect　n. 建筑师
②governor　n. 省长
③pagoda　n. 宝塔
④inspect　v.t. 检察,视察

swaying a little and asked why. The master builder explained that the upper① part was still light because the roof② tiles③ had not been put on.

Then, the tiles were all put on, but the top floor still swayed as before. Being at a loss④ as to what to do, the master builder privately⑤ sent his wife to offer Yu Hao's wife a present of golden hairpins⑥ so as to enquire⑦ about the cause of the swaying.

When Yu Hao's wife asked her husband to explain it, he laughed and said: "That's easy. They just need to nail in some struts⑧ and it will no longer sway."

After Yu Hao's wife told the master builder's wife, the master builder followed Yu

---

①upper　adj. 在上的,上部的
②roof　n. 屋顶,屋盖
③tile　n. 瓦(片)
④at a loss　困惑,不知所措
⑤privately　adv. 暗中,秘密地
⑥hairpin　n. 钗,夹发簪
⑦enquire　v.i. 查问
⑧strut　n. 支杆

Hao's advice and the tower stood quite firm. This is because the nailed struts braced① the structure, so that the six planes② [above and below, front and back, left and right] were connected together like a box. People walked on the struts, and the six planes still supported each other. There was no more swaying. Everybody acknowledged③ the expertise④ thus shown.

---

①brace v.t. 支柱,撑牢
②plane n. 平面
③acknowledge v.t. 承认
④expertise n. 专门技术

画蛇添足

[古文]

楚有祠者，赐其舍人卮①酒。舍人相谓曰："数人饮之不足，一人饮之有余。请画地为蛇，先成者饮酒。"一人蛇先成，引酒而饮之，乃左手持卮，右手画蛇，曰："吾能为之足！"未成！一人之蛇成，夺其卮，曰："蛇固无足，子安能为之足？"遂饮其酒。为蛇足者，终亡②其酒。

——《战国策》

[今译]

有个楚国人，在祭祖以后，把一大杯酒赐给他的门客们。门客中有人说："这杯酒供大家喝是不够的，给一人喝倒是多了些。我建议:各人在地上画条蛇，谁先画好，谁就喝这杯酒。"有个门客先画毕蛇，拿来酒杯打算喝。他左手拿着酒杯；右手一面继续画蛇，一面说："我给蛇添上

---

① 卮(zhī)：喝酒的用具。
② 亡：失去,丢失。

足。"当他正在给蛇添足时，另一个人已把蛇画好了，一把夺过酒杯说："蛇生来就没有足，你怎么能给蛇添足呢?"说完，就一饮而尽。那个画蛇添足的人，终于没有喝到酒。

[英译]

Adding Feet to the Snake①

A native of Chu, after worshipping② his ancestors③, gave his retainers④ a goblet⑤ of wine. One of the retainers said:

" It's insufficient⑥ for all of us, but too much for one of us. I suggest, therefore, that everybody draw⑦ a snake on the ground and the one who finishes drawing first will win the goblet of wine."

---

①snake n. 蛇
②worship v.t. 祭,礼拜
③ancestor n. 祖宗
④retainer n. 门客,侍从,家仆
⑤goblet n. 酒杯
⑥nsufficient adj. 不够的,不足的
⑦draw v.t. 画

When one retainer had completed his drawing, he took up the goblet to drink from it. As he held the goblet in his left hand, he continued to draw the snake with his right hand, saying:

"I'll add① some feet to it."

While he was adding feet to his snake, another man who had just then finished drawing his snake snatched② the pot from his hand, protesting③:

"No snake has feet. How can you add feet to it?"

Then he drank the wine. The man who added feet to the snake lost his prize④ in the end.

---

①add　v.t.　加,添加
②snatch　v.t.　抢夺
③protest　v.t.　抗议
④prize　n.　奖赏

痴人说梦

[古文]

　　戚某幼耽① 读而性痴。一日早起，谓婢某曰："尔昨夜梦见我否？"答曰："未。"大斥曰："梦中分明见尔，何矢赖？"往诉母曰："痴该打。我昨夜梦见他，他坚说未梦见我，岂有此理耶！"

——《笑笑录》

[今译]

　　有个姓戚的人，从小是个书呆子，傻里傻气。一天早晨起床后，对女佣人说："你昨天晚上梦见我了吗？"女佣人回答说："没有。"他大声呵叱说："我在梦里清清楚楚地看见你，怎么还抵赖呢？"他去告诉母亲说："这傻丫头真该打！我昨天晚上梦见她，她坚持说没有梦见我，真是岂有此理！"

---

① 耽(dān)：迟延。

It Takes a Fool① to

Talk Twaddle②

Once there was a man named Qi who was a bookworm③ ever since he was little. As a result, he was sort of a fool.

One day after he got up in the early morning, he asked his maidservant④:

"Did you see me in your dreams last night?"

"No," she replied.

'I saw you in my dreams. There is no mistake about that," he reproached⑤. "How dare you deny⑥ it?"

Then he went to complain⑦ to his mother:

---

①fool   n. 愚人，痴人
②twaddle   n. 愚蠢的话
③bookworm   n. 书呆子,蛀书虫
④maidservant   n. 女仆
⑤reproach   v.t. 责备,指责,非难
⑥deny   v.t. 否认
⑦complain   v.i. 抱怨,诉苦

"That stupid① maid ought to be punished②. I saw her in my dreams last night, but she maintains③ that she didn't see me. What utter nonsense④!"

---

①stupid   adj. 愚蠢的
②punish   v.t. 惩罚
③maintain   v.t. 坚持,强调
④nonsense   n. 胡说,完全胡说,岂有此理

嗟来之食

[古文]

　　齐大饥，黔敖为食于路，以待饿者而食之。有饿者，蒙袂①辑屦②，贸贸然来。黔敖左奉食，右执饮，曰："嗟!来食。"扬其目而视之曰："予唯不食嗟来之食，以至于斯也!"从而谢焉。终不食而死。

　　　　　　　　　——《礼记·檀弓下》

[今译]

　　齐国有一次闹大饥荒。黔敖在路边摆设饮食摊，施舍给饥饿者吃。有个饿汉有气无力地走来，他用衣袖蒙住脸；右手提着鞋子，似乎饿得连穿鞋的力气都没有了。当他摇摇晃晃地走来，停步在黔敖的饮食摊时，黔敖左手拿着吃的，右手拿着饮料，说："喂，过来吃!"这饿汉举目向他瞧了一眼说："我正因为不吃嗟来食，才弄到这般

―――――――――

①袂(mèi)：袖子
②辑屦(jíjú)：拖着鞋子。

地步的。"于是黔敖赶上去，对刚才的不礼貌,向他道歉。但这饿汉还是不肯吃，终于活活饿死了。

[英译]

Food Given in an

Impolite① Manner

There once was a severe② famine③ in Qi. Qian Ao had food ready at the roadside for the starvelings④ to eat. A famished man staggered⑤ up. He covered his face with his sleeve because of shame, and carried his shoes in hand as he was too weak to wear them. He was halted⑥ by Qian Ao, who held food in his left hand and drink in the right, saying:

---

①impolite adj. 没礼貌的,粗鲁的
②severe adj. 严重的
③famine n. 饥荒
④starveling n .挨饿者
⑤stagger v.i. 摇晃,蹒跚
⑥halt v.t. 止步,停止

"Hey you, come and eat!"

The man raised① his eyes and looked at him. "I have become thus only because I don't want to eat anything given in such a rude manner." he said.

So, following him, Qian Ao made an immediate apology② to him for not being so polite at first, but still the man refused to take any food and died of hunger in the end.

---

①raise v.t. 举起
②apology n. 道歉

悔 改 篇

The Chapter of Repentance

裴矩进谏

[古文]

上患吏多受赇①，密使左右试略之。有司门令史受绢一匹，上欲杀之，民部尚书裴矩谏曰："为吏受略，罪诚当死；但陛下使人遗之而受，乃陷人于法也，恐非所谓'道之以德，齐之以礼'。"上悦，召文武五品以上告之曰："裴矩能当官力争，不为面从，傥②每事皆然，何忧不治！"

—— 司马光 《资治通鉴》

[今译]

唐太宗忧虑朝廷中许多官吏接受贿赂，就暗暗派手下亲信试着去贿赂他们。有个掌管门房的小官接受了一匹绢，太宗想杀了他。民部尚书裴矩进谏说："当官的接受贿赂，固然罪该处死。但这次是陛下派人送给他，他才接受的。这样做是陷害别人犯法，恐怕不符合古人所讲的'用道德

———————

①赇(qiú)：贿赂
②傥(tǎng)：假如。

教导人，用礼节制约人'的道理吧。"太宗听了很高兴，召集五品以上的文武官员，告诉他们说："裴矩能当面据理力争，不搞当面顺从那一套，假如每件事都能这样，还愁国家治不好吗？"

Pei Ju's Admonition①

Tang Taizong [the first Emperor of the Tang Dynasty]was perturbed② about government officials who took bribes. So once he sent his intimates③ to bribe them secretly in order to test them. When a lower official in charge of the capital gate accepted a roll④ of cloth as a bribe, the Emperor decided to execute⑤ him.

Pei Ju, the senior official of civil administra-

---

①admonition　n. 告诫,劝告
②perturb　v.t. 使不安
③intimate　n. 亲信
④roll　n. 卷(轴); a roll of cloth 一匹布
⑤execute　v.t. 将…处死

tion①, admonished② the Emperor not to do it:
"All officials who take bribes deserve to be exe-
cuted. But this time the bribe was surely sent by
Your Majesty③, so the official took it. As such
an action is in fact a way to trick④
somebody into violating⑤ the law, it probably
goes against the motto⑥: Teaching people with
morality⑦; restricting⑧ them with politeness."

On hearing it, the Emperor felt pleased and
gathered together the civil⑨ and military⑩ officials above the fifth rank⑪ and said:

"Being an official, Pei Ju can argue strongly
on just grounds⑫ ,   and he doesn't just

---

①administration n. 行政机关：civil administration 民政
②admonish v.t. 劝告：admonish sb. to do sth. 劝某人做某事
③majesty n. 陛下
④trick v.t. 欺，骗
⑤violate v.t. 违反：violate the law 犯法
⑥motto n. 箴言
⑦morality n. 道德
⑧restrict v.t. 限制,约束
⑨civil adj. 文职的,文官的
⑩military adj. 军职的,军事的
⑪rank n. 等级
⑫argue strongly on just grounds 据理力争

submit① to my wishes because of my presence. If everything is done this way, need we be afraid of being unable to administer② our country?"

---

①submit   v.i.   服从
②administer   v.t.   管理,治理

宋太祖怕史官

[古文]

太祖常弹雀于后苑，有群臣称有急事请见；太祖见之，其所奏乃常事。上怒，诘① 其故。对曰："臣以为尚急于弹雀。"上愈怒，以柱斧柄撞其口，堕两齿。其人徐俯拾齿置于怀。上曰："汝怀齿，欲讼② 我耶？"对曰："臣不能讼陛下，自有史官书之。"上悦，赐金帛。

—— 司马光 《涑水纪闻》

[今译]

宋太祖有一次在后花园拿弹弓打小鸟雀，忽然臣下报告有急事面奏。宋太祖接见了他，不料这个人所说的却是一般的例行公事。宋太祖怒气冲冲，责问臣下为什么要报说"急事"。臣下回答说："我认为它总比用弹弓打鸟来得要紧些吧。"宋太祖更加恼怒，用长斧柄撞他的嘴，竟把两颗牙齿打落下来。这个人慢慢地弯下腰捡起牙齿藏在

---

① 诘：盘问
② 讼：诉讼。

怀里。宋太祖说："你藏起牙齿，难道想留着告我的状吗？"他回答说："我怎能告陛下？这件事今后自有史官直笔记下的。"宋太祖转怒为喜，便赏给他一些金帛。

[英译]

Emperor Song Taizu Fearing

the Historiographer①

One day when Emperor Song Taizu was shooting sparrows② with a slingshot③ in his back garden, some of his officials reported that there was a man who asked to see him, saying that he had an urgent matter to report. The Emperor received him, but found his report only concerned a routine④ matter. Becoming angry with him, the Emperor asked him why he did so.

---

①historiographer n. 史官
②sparrow n. 麻雀
③slingshot n. 弹弓
④routine n. 例行公事

"I thought it was more important than shooting sparrows," replied the official.

The Emperor got even angrier and he struck① the official on mouth with the handle of his long ax②. As a result, two of his teeth fell out. The official slowly crouched③ down to pick up his teeth and hid them in his breast④ pocket.

"Why are you keeping your teeth?" asked the Emperor, "Are you going to enter a lawsuit⑤against me?"

"How could I bring in a lawsuit against Your Majesty? The historiographer will note it down outright⑥."

On hearing it, the Emperor went from angry to pleased and gifted him with some gold and silk.

---

①strike (struck, striken) v.t. 打,撞
②ax (复 axes) n. 斧
③crouch n. 低头弯腰,蹲下
④breast n. (衣服的)胸部
⑤lawsuit n. 诉讼(案件): enter (或 bring in) a lawsuit against sb. 对某人起诉
⑥outright adv. 直率地,全部地

七步成诗

[古文]

　　文帝① 尝令东阿王② 七步中作诗，不成者行大法。应声便为诗曰："煮豆燃豆萁，豆在釜中泣。本自同根生，相煎何太急!"帝深有惭色。

　　　　　　　　——刘义庆　《世说新语》

[今译]

　　曹丕曾命令曹植在七步内写一首诗，写不成就要对他施严刑重法。曹植当即念了一首诗道："锅里煮豆子，锅底下烧豆茎，豆子在锅里哭泣，豆茎、豆子都是同一条根上长出来的，豆茎何必要急不可耐地煎熬豆子呢!"曹丕听了，顿觉非常惭愧。

---

①文帝：指曹丕,三国时魏国的建立者,文学家,曹操的儿子。
②东阿王：指曹植,三国时魏国诗人，曹操的儿子。

Verses① Composed in

Seven Paces

One day Emperor Wendi (Cao Pi) ordered his brother, Cao Zhi, to compose② a poem in seven paces③.

"If you fail to do it," said the Emperor, "You will be severely punished." Then Cao Zhi immediately recited a poem aloud:

The kettle④ had beans⑤ inside,
And stalks⑥ of the beans made the fire;
The beans to the brother-stalks cried,

"*We sprang⑦ from one root, why such ire⑧?*"

---

①verse n. 一行诗,一首诗词或韵文
②compose v.t. 作(诗、歌、文)
③pace n. 步
④kettle n. 锅,壶
⑤bean n. 豆
⑥stalk n. 杆,秸
⑦spring (sprang, sprung) v.i. 生出,长出来
⑧ire n. (诗中用)怒气,发火

On hearing it, the Emperor was much ashamed of himself.

停建中天台

[古文]

　　魏王将起中天台，令曰："敢谏者死！"许绾负操锸①入，曰："闻大王将起中天台，臣愿加一力！"王曰："子何力有加？"绾曰："虽无力，能商台。"王曰："若何？"曰："臣闻天与地相去万五千里，今王因而半之，当起七千五百里台。高既如此，其趾须方八千里，尽王之地，不足以为台趾。……王必起此台，先以兵伐诸侯，尽有其地，犹不足，又伐四夷，……乃足以为台趾。材木之积，人徒之众！仓廪之储，数以万亿，……当定农亩之地，足以奉给王之台者，台具以备，乃可以作。"魏王默然无以应，乃罢起台。

　　　　　　　——刘向　《新序·刺奢》

[今译]

　　魏王心血来潮，决定造一座很高很高的中天台。他下令："有敢劝阻者，杀无赦。"许绾听到这个消息，扛着一把铁锹去见魏王说："听说大王要

————————

①锸(chā)：铁锹。

造中天台，我愿意尽一把力!"魏王说:"象你这样的人，能出什么力呢?"许缩说:"我虽然力气不大，但是为了造中天台，我是能够出一把力的。听说：天地相隔一万五千里，中天台有半个天高，就得有七千五百里。这样高的台，台基就得占方圆八千里的土地，否则台就立不住。现在魏国的全部国土，还不够修个台基，所以先要出兵去打邻国，占有他们的土地。可能还不够用，只好派兵去打那些远在天涯海角的国家。有了台基，还得有土地给造台的人住。再说，堆粮食、堆木料也要土地。说远一点，还要有块更大的土地种粮食给造台的人吃。有那么多的事，要人去干，我怎么会没有地方去出力呢?所以我就扛着铁锹来听您的差遣了。"魏王一句话都说不出来了。他收回成命，不造中天台了。

[英译]

No Mid-sky Tower is to be Built

Once the King of the State of Wei, acting on a sudden impulse①, decided to build an

---

①impulse n. 冲动,兴奋

extremely high tower and even had a name for it
—" Mid—sky Tower." He issued① a decree②:
" Anyone who dared come to advise the King
against his plan should be killed."

Xu Wan, despite this, went to see the King
with a spade③ on his shoulder. " I hear that
Your Majesty wants to build a Mid—sky Tower,
so I've come to do my duty."

"What work can you do in this construction?" said the King.

"Though I'm not young and strong, I think
I'm still able to do something in the construction." "How so?" the King said. " I have
heard that our earth is fifteen thousand li from
the sky. If the Mid—sky Tower is to be half that
height, it will have to be seven thousand five
hundred li high. Now, such a high tower should
have a base at least eight thousand square li,
[otherwise the tower would certainly collapse④].

---

①issue   v.t. 发布
②decree   n. 政令，法令
③spade   n. 铁锹,铲
④collapse   v.i. 倒坍

At present, our domain① is not big enough for the base of the tower. We should conquer the neighbouring states first. But it is quite possible that their territories② would still not be spacious③ enough for this base, so the only way out is to send troops to conquer the states in the remotest④ corners of the earth. In addition, we should provide land for the builders to live on, land to store grain and stack⑤ timber. Moreover, a still wider area is needed to plant crops for the builders. So many projects are to be done! I think that in any case you may find me useful in your construction. This is why I've come with a spade to see Your Majesty."

The King of Wei, who was left speechless, rescinded⑥ his order —— no tower would be built.

---

①domain   n. 领土,势力圈
②territory   n. 领土,领地
③spacious   adj. 广阔的
④remote   adj. 遥远的
⑤stack   v.t. 堆起,堆积; n. 堆,大量
⑥rescind   v.t. 撤回,取消

讽 喻 篇

The Chapter of Allegory

枭将东徙

[古文]

　　枭逢鸠，鸠曰："子将安之？"枭曰："我将东徙。"鸠曰："何故？"枭曰："乡人皆恶我鸣，以故东徙。"鸠曰："子能更鸣，可矣；不能更鸣，东徙犹恶① 子之声。"

　　　　　　——刘向　《说苑·说丛》

[今译]

　　猫头鹰碰见斑鸠，斑鸠问它："你要到哪里去呀？"猫头鹰说："我准备搬到东边去。"斑鸠问："为什么呢？"猫头鹰说："村里人都讨厌我的叫声，因此，我想搬到东边去。"斑鸠说："你能改变你的叫声，搬到东边去是可以的；如果不能改变你的叫声，搬到东边去，东边村里人照样讨厌你的叫声。"

---

①恶：讨厌

An Owl① Moving to the East

Once an owl chanced upon a turtle—dove②
on his way.

" Where are you going?" asked the
turtle—dove.

"I am moving to the east," replied the owl.

"Why?"

" Because all the villagers③ here dislike④
the way I cry."

" That won't be a problem if you could
change it. If not, people in the east will
hate⑤ to hear your cries just the same⑥."

---

①owl n. 猫头鹰,枭; adj. 深夜活动的:an owl train 夜间行
　驶的火车; an owl show 深夜演出的电影或戏剧
②turtle—dove n. 斑鸠,雉鸠
③villager n. 村民,村人
④dislike v.t. 厌恶
⑤hate v.t. 憎恨,嫌恶
⑥just the same 完全一样

医人治驼

[古文]

昔有医人，自媒①能治背驼，曰:“如弓者，如虾者，如曲环者，延②吾治，可朝治而夕如矢③。”一人信焉，而使治驼。乃索板二片，以一置地下，卧驼者其上，又以一压焉，而即蹝[1]焉，驼者随直，亦复随死。

——江盈科　《雪涛小说》

[今译]

从前有个医生，自称专治驼背。他说:“无论驼得像弓、像虾、像曲环的人，请我来治疗，早上开始治，晚上就把背治得像箭那样直。”有个驼背人相信了他的话，就跑去请他医治。于是这个医生拿出两块木板。他把一块放在地上，叫驼背

---

①媒：介绍。

②延：聘请;邀请。

③矢：箭

④蹝(xǐ)：鞋

人趴在板上，另一块压在他身子上。然后他拖着鞋子在木板上乱蹦乱跳。结果驼背虽然压直了，但驼背人也被压死了。

[英译]

Curing the Hunchback①

A certain doctor claimed he could cure hunchbacks.

"I specialize② in curing hunchbacks of all kinds," said the doctor, "whether bowshaped③, shrimp−shaped④, or circular⑤. My cure will instantly make them right straight."

A hunchback who believed what that doctor said came to the doctor to be cured. The doctor took out two planks⑥, one of which he placed on the ground for the patient to lie on and the other

---

①hunchback n. 驼背
②specialize v.i. (in) 专门研究
③bow−shaped adj. 弓形的
④shrimp−shaped adj. 虾形的
⑤circular adj. 圆圈的
⑥plank n. 厚木板

he put on the patient's body to have him
sandwiched①. Afterwards, he slipped② into his
shoes, jumped onto the plank and began jumping
wildly. The hunchback died in the end, though
his hunchback was indeed set straight.

---

①sandwich　v.t. (between) 紧夹于中间
②slip (slipped)　v.i. (into or out of) 匆忙地(穿或脱)

外科医生

[古文]

　　有医者，自称善外科。一裨①将阵回，中流矢，深入膜内，延使治。乃持并州剪，剪去矢管②，跪而请谢。裨将曰："镞③在膜④内者，须亟治。"医曰："此内科事，不意并责我。"

　　　　　　　——江盈科　《雪涛小说》

[今译]

　　有个医生，自吹精通外科。一次有个副将从战场回来，身上中了箭，箭头射进皮肉里面，便请这个医生治疗。医生拿出一把并州出产的锋利的剪刀，一下子将露在皮肉外面的箭杆剪掉，然后跪在副将面前请求赏赐。副将说："箭头还留在皮肉里面，必须赶快治疗。"医生说："这是内科医

---

①裨：副，偏。
②管：此指箭杆。
③镞：指箭头。
④膜：皮肤。

—218—

生的事，想不到也一起要我治疗。"

[英译]

The Surgeon[①]

A certain doctor called himself a very fine surgeon. So, after returning from the battlefield, a vice-general who was pierced by an arrow that went deep into his flesh[②] came to see the doctor for treatment[③]. The doctor took out a pair of sharp scissors[④] which were made in Bingzhou.

"Crack!" The arrow shaft[⑤] snapped[⑥]. The doctor grovelled[⑦] before the wounded officer and asked for a reward[⑧]

"But the arrowhead is still in my flesh!" said

---

①surgeon　n. 外科医生
②flesh　n. 肌肉
③treatment　n. 治疗
④scissors　n. pl. 剪刀
⑤shaft　n. 箭杆
⑥snap　v.i. 突然折断
⑦grovel　v.i. 跪
⑧reward　n. 报酬

the military man, " It is necessary to cure the wound at once."

"The wound inside your flesh must be taken care of by a doctor of internal medicine①, not a surgeon," replied the doctor. "I don't think it's my duty to do anything about it."

---

① internal medicine 内科

半 日 闲

[古文]

　　有贵人游僧舍，酒酣，诵唐人诗云："因过竹院逢僧话，又得浮生①半日闲。"僧闻而笑之。贵人问僧何笑，僧曰："尊官得半日闲，老僧却忙了三日。"

　　　　　　——冯梦龙　《古今谭概》

[今译]

　　有个大官到寺院去游玩，酒喝到畅快的时候，朗诵起唐人的诗句："因过竹院逢僧话，又得浮生半日闲。"和尚听了发笑。大官问和尚为什么发笑。和尚说："贵官固然消闲了半日，我这老和尚可整整忙了三天！"

---

①浮生：谓世事无定生命短促。

A Half-day's Rest

A high official once went sight-seeing① to a temple②. Enjoying this trip, he drank like a fish③ and began to recite verses④ from a famous poet of the Tang Dynasty:

How I enjoyed the half-day's rest
In a courtyard⑤ deep in a bamboo grove⑥,
Where I had an interesting talk
With the noble monk I met.

On hearing these verses, the old monk burst into laughter⑦.

"Is anything funny⑧ enough to make you laugh like that?" the high official asked the old monk.

---

①sight-seeing n. 观光,游览
②temple n. 寺院,庙宇
③drink like a fish 畅饮
④verse n. 诗,韵文
⑤courtyard n. 庭院
⑥bamboo grove 竹林
⑦burst into laughter 突然大笑
⑧funny adj. 有趣的,好玩的

"You have enjoyed a half-day's rest, while I, an old monk, have been busy for three whole days!"

狐假虎威

[古文]

　　虎求百兽而食之，得狐。狐曰："子无敢食我也!天帝使我长百兽，今子食我，是逆天帝命也。子以我为不信，吾为子先行，子随我后，观百兽之见我而敢不走乎?"虎以为然，故遂与之行，兽见之皆走，虎不知兽畏己而走也，以为畏狐也。

　　　　　　　　　　——《战国策》

[今译]

　　一天，老虎寻找各种动物吃，他抓住了一只狐狸。狐狸对老虎说："你不敢吃我!上帝任命我当百兽之长。现在你吃我，这是违背上帝的意志。如果你不相信我的话，可以让我走在你的前面，你跟在我的后面。看哪个动物见了我而敢不跑?"老虎认为狐狸说得有理，就跟随狐狸同走。群兽一见到他俩都吓跑了。老虎不知道群兽是害怕它才跑的，却以为群兽是害怕狐狸才跑的。

The Fox Borrowing the

Tiger's Terror①

A tiger went about② in search of ③ other weaker animals for food. Once in his hunting④, he happened to find a fox.

"You won't dare to eat me," said the fox, "as I am appointed⑤ by God to be the head of all animals. It is against the will of God if you eat me now. In case⑥ you don't believe what I say, let us go together. You just follow me and see whether there is any animal that doesn't run away when I pass."

The tiger agreed and went with the fox. Certainly he saw all the animals run away upon seeing the fox. He thought they were afraid of the

---

①terror　n. 恐怖,惊骇
②go about　四处走动
③in search of 寻找,搜索
④hunt　v.i. 搜索,打猎
⑤appoint　v.t. 任命,选派
⑥in case　假使,如果,免得,以防(万一)

fox without knowing it was he himself that they feared.

一窍不通

[古文]

　　昔年陈……　侍郎兰彬，出使美国.有随员徐某，夙① 不解西文。一日，持西报展览颇入神。使馆译员见之，讶② 然曰："君何时谙识西文乎?"徐曰："我固不谙。"译员曰："君既不谙西文，阅此奚为?"徐答曰："余以为阅西文固不解，阅诸君之翻译文亦不解。同一不解，固不如阅西文之为愈也。"

　　　　——辜鸿铭　《张文襄幕府纪闻》

[今译]

　　从前，陈兰彬当副部长时，有一次赴美国访问。在随行人员中有个姓徐的，他平素对英文一窍不通。一天，他拿了英文报佯装看得全神贯注。大使馆的译员见了，十分惊奇地问："您什么时候懂英文啦?"

---

①夙·　平常,平素。
②讶·　惊奇,诧异。

"我当然不懂英文。"徐某说。

"您既然不懂英文，为什么看英文报纸呢?"译员问。

徐某答道:"我认为:我固然看不懂英文，但也看不懂你们翻译的中文;既然英文和译文都看不懂，还不如看英文的好些。"

[英译]

Both Are Greek to Me①

Many years ago a Mr. Xu was in the suite② of Chen Lanbin, a vice minister who at that time had been sent on a mission③ to the USA. Though quite ignorant④ of English, once Mr. Xu was pretending⑤ to read an English newspaper with absorbing⑥ interest. The interpreter

---

①It is (all) Greek to me.　我一窍不通
②suite　n. (一批)随从人员
③be sent on a mission　出使
④ignorant　adj. 无知的
⑤pretend　vt. 假装,装做
⑥absorbing　adj. 专心的

of the legation① who had witnessed② the scene asked him in surprise:

"When did you learn English?"

"I have not yet learned it," the other replied.

"Since you don't know English, why on earth should you be reading the paper?" the interpreters went on.

"I cannot understand English," answered Mr. Xu quietly, "nor can I understand your translation. So I think it's better to read the original than to read your translations, because both are Greek to me."

---

①legation n. 公使馆
②witness v.t. 目睹

止母念佛

[古文]

翟母皈心释氏，日诵佛不辍① 声。(翟)永龄
佯呼之，母应诺，又呼不已，母愠曰："无有，何
频呼也？"永龄曰："吾呼母三四，母便不悦，彼佛
者日为母呼千万声，其怒当何如？"母为少悟。

———— 浮白斋主人 《雅谑》

[今译]

翟永龄的母亲信奉佛教,每天不停地念佛
经。翟永龄假装有事呼唤她，她应了一声；翟永
龄又不停声地呼唤，她生气地说"没有事情，干
嘛喊个不停！"翟永龄说："我只喊了你三四声，你
就不高兴了，那菩萨每天被你呼喊千万声，他该
多恼怒啊！"翟母这才有些醒悟。

①辍：停止。

Preventing Mother From[①]

Chanting[②] Scriptures[③]

After she was converted[④] to Buddhism[⑤], not for a day did Zhai Yongling's mother ever stop chanting scriptures and invoking[⑥] the name of Buddha[⑦]. It was too much for Yong—ling, so he purposely[⑧] started calling "Mother!" pretending he had something to say to her. His mother answered "yes?" He called again and his mother answered again. This went on and on till the old lady got irritated[⑨] and cried:

" Why do you repeatedly call me like a fool?"

---

①prevent ... from　阻止,使…不,防止…以免
②chant　v.t. 单调地唱(或说)
③scripture　n. 经典,经文
④convert　v.t. 使皈依宗教
⑤Buddhism　n. 佛教,释教
⑥invoke　v.t. 祈求(神灵)保佑,乞灵于
⑦Buddha　n. 佛,如来佛,佛陀
⑧purposely　adv. 故意地,特意地
⑨irritate　v.t. 激怒,使恼怒

The son retorted①: "I have only done it a few times, yet you soon became irritated. How much angrier would Buddha be when you call upon Him thousands of times a day?"

Hearing it, the old lady somewhat② realized her own foolery③.

①retort v.t. 反驳
②somewhat adv. 有点,稍微
③foolery n. 愚蠢的行为

阉　羊

[古文]

艾子蓄羊两头于圈①，羊牡者好斗，每遇生人，则逐而触之。门人辈往来，甚以为患，请于艾子曰：“夫子之羊牡而猛，请得阉之，则降其性而驯矣！”艾子笑曰：“尔不知今日无阳道的更猛里！”

——陆灼　《艾子后语》

[今译]

艾子在后园里养了两只羊，公羊喜欢角斗，每遇见陌生人，便赶上去用角撞人。他的学生来来往往，都提心吊胆的，于是同艾子商议：“老师，你的公羊生性凶猛，请允许我们把它阉了，它就会变得温顺了！”艾子笑了笑说：“你们不知道，如今阉了的，不是更凶猛吗？”

---

①圈(yòu)：蓄养牲畜的地方。

Castration① Does Not Help

Master Ai kept two goats② in his yard. The male one, born hostile③, would butt④ any stranger that came in its way.

Master Ai's disciples⑤, coming and going everyday, found it very troublesome⑥, and so they proposed⑦ to their teacher:

"Master, your billy-goat is fierce⑧ by nature⑨. Please allow us to castrate it to subdue⑩ its temper⑪, and it will soon be tamed⑫."

Master Ai smiled and said:

---

①castration n. 阉割 castrate v.t.
②goat n. 山羊,公羊
③hostile adj. 敌意的,敌对的,不友善的
④butt v.t. 顶撞,碰撞
⑤disciple n. 弟子,信徒
⑥troublesome adj. 讨厌的,令人烦恼的,麻烦的
⑦propose v.t. (to) 提议,建议,提出
⑧fierce adj. 凶猛的,残忍的
⑨by nature 天生地,天性地
⑩subdue v.t. 使驯服,使屈服,征服
⑪temper n. 脾气,性情,情绪,心情
⑫tame v.t. 驯服

"Don't you know that nowadáys① those devoid② of manly③ ways behave④ even more fiercely?"

---

①nowadays　adv. 如今,现在
②devoid　adj. (of) 没有
③manly　adj. 男子气概的,果断的,适合男子的
④behave　v.i. 举止,表现,举动

说谎老君

[古文]

　　太上老君云:"诵经千遍,身腾紫云。"道士笃信此说,诵至九百九十九遍,乃沐浴登坛①,告别亲友,俟②候腾云。更诵一遍辏③千数,至暮竟无片云。道士指老君塑像叹曰:"谁知你这等老大年纪也会说谎。"

　　　　　　　——冯梦龙　《广笑府》

〔今译〕

　　太上老君说:"读经千遍,身子就能够腾云驾雾。"一个道士深信此说,读到九百九十九遍,就洗澡净身,登上祭台,告别亲友,等候腾云。又读了一遍凑成千数,到晚上竟然没有一片云出现。道士指着老君的塑像叹口气说:"谁知道你这么大岁数也会说谎话。"

---

①坛: 土筑的高台,用于盟誓、祭祀。
②俟(sì): 等待。
③辏(còu): 聚集。此是凑集成……。

Laojun Telling a Lie①

Taishang Laojun [the father of Taoism②] was heard to have said: "[If anyone were to hold fast to③ his faith, say] by chanting the Taoist scriptures a thousand times, he would rise into the purple clouds of Heaven④."

Foolishly following his words, a Taoist monk started chanting until the nine hundred and ninety-ninth time. Then he cleansed⑤ his body in a bath and mounted⑥ a sacrificial⑦ terrace⑧, bidding⑨ farewell⑩ to his relatives⑪

---

①tell a lie 说谎
②Taoism n. 道教
③hold fast to 坚持
④rise into the purple clouds of Heaven 腾云驾雾
⑤cleanse v.t. 使清洁,清洗
⑥mount v.t. 登上
⑦sacrificial adj. 祭祀的
⑧terrace n. 露台,平台,阳台
⑨bid(bade / bid, bidden) v.t. 表示
⑩farewell n. 告别,告别话
⑪relative n. 亲属,亲戚

and friends and waiting for the lift. [Everything ready,]he chanted once more to make up the round number of① one thousand. Evening came. Yet not a trace② of clouds had appeared in the sky.

Pointing his finger at a statue③ of Taishang Laojun, he heaved④ a sigh⑤ of dejection⑥:

" Who would know that one of your senior⑦ age could also tell a lie!"

---

①make up the round number of… 凑足整数
②trace 痕迹,丝毫,微量: a trace of clouds 一片云
③statue n. 塑像
④heave (heaved / hove) v.t. 发出(叹息)
⑤sigh n. 叹息、叹气
⑥dejection n. 沮丧,情绪低落
⑦senior adj. 年长的,年纪较长的

黔 之 驴

[古文]

　　黔无驴，有好事者，船载以人；至则无可用，放之山下。虎见之，庞然大物也，以为神；蔽林间窥之。稍出，近之，慭慭①然莫相知。他日驴一鸣，虎大骇，远遁，以为且噬己也，甚恐。然往来视之，觉无异能者。益习其声，又进出前后，终不敢搏。稍近益狎，荡倚冲冒；驴不胜怒，蹄之。虎因喜，计之曰："技止此耳。"因跳踉大㘎②，断其喉，尽其肉，乃去。

　　　　　　——柳宗元　《柳河东集》

[今译]

　　贵州一向没有驴子。有个爱管闲事的人，用船装载了一头驴子，运到贵州时，他觉得驴子对他一无用处。于是就把它放生山脚下。有只老虎见了驴子，认为这巨大的东西是个神灵。起初，

---

① 慭慭(yìn)：小心谨慎的样子。
② 㘎(hǎn)：虎叫声。

老虎隐蔽在树林里偷偷观望驴子。接着，老虎战战兢兢地走出树林，朝驴子方向走去，但是不敢靠近驴子。有一天，驴子鸣叫了一声，老虎吓得远远逃走，十分害怕，担心驴子会吃掉它。后来，老虎又跑了回来，从四面八方仔细观察驴子，发现它并没有什么特殊的本领。老虎渐渐听惯了驴子的叫声，靠近驴子再也不感到恐惧，但还是不敢去碰撞驴子。然而，老虎愈来愈壮着胆去亲近、戏弄、触怒驴子，试试它有多大本领。驴子生气极了，用蹄子去踢老虎。这时老虎心中大喜，因为他估计出驴子的本领不过如此。于是，它大吼一声，向驴子猛扑过去，先咬断驴子的喉咙，再把它的肉吃得精光，然后扬长而去。

[英译]

The Ass[①] Brought to Guizhou

There was no ass in Guizhou. Some busybody[②] brought in one by boat. But when the ass arrived, this person found he could make

---

① ass n. 驴子
② busybody n. 好事的人，爱管闲事的人

no use of it, so he left it at the foot of a mountain.

Seeing it, a tiger thought such a huge thing must be none other than a god. At first he peeped① at it from behind the woods, and then moved timidly② towards it; but still he dared not get too near it.

One day the ass brayed③, and the tiger was so frightened that he ran miles away for fear it was going to eat him up. Later on he came back to look at it from all quarters④ and found it possessed no particular ability. Though he, being more accustomed⑤ to its braying, was no longer afraid to come near it, he still dared not attack it. He ventured⑥ to tease⑦ it more and more with a view to testing its abilities. Being greatly angry, the ass gave·him a kick. By now

---

①peep　v.i. 偷看,窥视
②timidly　adv. 胆怯地
③bray　v.i. (驴)叫
④from all quarters　从不同方向
⑤accustom　v.t. 使习惯
⑥venture　v.i. 冒…危险, 敢于
⑦tease　v.t. 戏弄

the tiger was very glad as he found it was at its wit's① end and had no ability other than this. Therefore, he roared and pounced② upon the ass, first breaking its neck and then eating up all its flesh, and went away.

---

①wit　n.　才智
②pounce　v.i.　猛扑

责任编辑：龙燕俐

封面设计：李法明

图书在版编目（CIP）数据

古文今译与英译/冯树鉴编译.-北京：华语教学出版社，2000.5

ISBN 7-80052-149-4

Ⅰ.古…Ⅱ.冯…Ⅲ.文言文-翻译Ⅳ.H159

中国版本图书馆 CIP 数据核字（2000）第 22532 号

古文今译与英译

编译　冯树鉴

＊

©华语教学出版社

华语教学出版社出版

（中国北京百万庄路 24 号）

邮政编码 100037

电话：(86) 10-68994599 / 68326333

传真：(86) 10-68326642

电子信箱：sinolingua@ihw.com.cn

北京星月印刷厂印刷

中国国际图书贸易总公司发行

（中国北京车公庄西路 35 号）

北京邮政信箱第 399 号　邮政编码 100044

新华书店国内发行

1990 年（40 开）第一版

2000 年第二次印刷

（汉英）

ISBN 7-80052-149-4 / H·150

定价：10.00 元

9—CE—2483P